YOUR LOVE STORY

YOUR LOVE STORY

A Guide to Engagement and Marriage

William Turrentine

COUPLE TO
COUPLE LEAGUE
LIVE THE LOVE

Publisher
Couple to Couple League International, Inc.

Mailing address
P.O. Box 111184
Cincinnati, OH 45211
800-745-8252, 513-471-2000
ccli@ccli.org

Nihil obstat
Sr. Paula Jean Miller, FSE
February 18, 2016

Imprimatur
Most Rev. Salvatore J. Cordileone
Archbishop of San Francisco
February 18, 2016

> The *Nihil obstat* and the *Imprimatur* are a declaration that a book or pamphlet is considered to be free from doctrinal or moral error. It is not implied that those who have granted the *Nihil obstat* and *Imprimatur* agree with the contents, opinions, or statements expressed.

Cataloging data
Library of Congress: 2015959476
ISBN: 978-0-926412-01-9

Turrentine, William
Your Love Story: A Guide to Engagement and Marriage
1. Marriage   2. Christian marriage   3. Sacraments
4. Marriage counseling   5. Marriage preparation

With gratitude for St. Thomas Aquinas,
who teaches us about Divine Love,
and
St. John Paul II,
who teaches us about
human love that reflects Divine Love

I ask you . . . to be revolutionaries . . . to rebel against this culture that sees everything as temporary and that ultimately believes you are incapable of responsibility, that believes you are incapable of true love. I have confidence in you and I pray for you.

Have the courage to swim against the tide.
And also have the courage to be happy.

—Pope Francis

Note to the Reader

With permission, the real names of the couples and the two priests who contributed their stories have been used. The names in the anecdotal examples are fictional.

CONTENTS

A Vocation to Love

The Most Reverend Salvatore J. Cordileone
Archbishop of San Francisco

GOD HAS DESIGNED EACH OF US to be conceived within the holy union of marriage between a man and a woman. Living your God-given call to marriage with faithfulness is the best gift you can give to your children and to the culture at large, since we develop our full human potential within the loving community of a family. It is there that we learn to love, to be in community with others, and it is there that we first learn our Faith.

Married Christian couples are called to be apostles of divine love made visible and tangible in our everyday world. In providing a living image of fidelity and fruitful love and by modeling the love of Jesus for his Church, sacramental marriages are essential to building a civilization based on truth and love. This sacrament, where "the two become one," has the power to transform not only your lives but the lives of all those around you. No solution to society's many problems will have a lasting effect unless we rebuild a culture of marriage and family.

Your Love Story will inform, encourage, and support you—as individuals and as married or engaged couples—to become living witnesses to the power of marriage that is faithful, permanent, and open to the gift of life. It draws together the ordinary and the extraordinary, the sacred and the secular, the sacrifices and the transcendent joys of marriage. Priests and deacons will find in it engaging ways to share the Church's teaching on love, sexuality, and marriage. Engaged and married couples will be intrigued, informed, and challenged.

We know that marriage is God's "original gift" to humanity, and when lived as He designed it, it is truly a taste of heaven. As you prepare yourself to stand before God on your wedding day and administer to each other the Sacrament of Marriage . . . and when you are being tried in the fires of everyday married life . . . remember the call of your vocation, to create this great civilization of truth and love, beginning in your own home and expanding to encompass those around you.

As you accept the honor bestowed upon you through God's call to this vocation of marriage, I pray you will receive the wisdom and the strength to live out the foundational truths of marriage and family, always proclaiming them with love and compassion. Let us call upon our God for the grace to go forth and do this together.

In fraternal union with your bishops, I offer you my love, affirmation, and support as you write your own love story based on the ultimate story of love—the story of our God, who *is* love.

Finding the Way Up

I KNOW AN ENGINEER WHO FREQUENTLY FLIES by helicopter between oil rigs in the Gulf of Mexico. He once explained to me that if a helicopter crashes in the water and sinks, its occupants can be so spun around that they become confused about up and down. They could swim with all their strength to reach the surface but might actually be swimming down. So, as part of his employer's requirement to practice survival skills, my engineer friend gets whirled around underwater in a simulator every year and practices a few tricks to tell which way is up, such as blowing little bubbles and following them to the surface.

If anyone was ever spun around about marriage, it was me. I was raised in Marin County, California. My family was loving but not religious, and I did not grow up with a belief in God. I was eager, however, to solve the riddle of existence. My elder brother, now deceased, had cerebral palsy and epilepsy and suffered a great deal. His suffering sent me on a search for the meaning of life. But I never considered looking in the direction of Christianity. I assumed that science had disproved the Bible, that belief in a personal God was merely a projection from our experience of having parents, and that the Crucifixion of Jesus was just another Roman execution. If anything, I considered myself a New Age, Zen Buddhist kind of guy.

My years in college coincided with the maximum intensity of the sexual revolution. It was an era when traditional ways of thinking were cast aside as unhealthy, and new, "liberated" approaches were adopted as natural and good. Sexual desire was to be celebrated, not repressed. The old-fashioned institution of marriage was obviously too narrow and needed reinvention for the dawning of a new age. The perfect living arrangement, it seemed to me, would be for men and (lots of) beautiful women to live together in communes, with the whole community responsible for raising any children.

My notion of the right way up then entered a period of radical readjustment, caused by two encounters with reality that definitely spun me in a different direction. The first happened while I was rock climbing with some friends in Yosemite Valley in 1971, the year I graduated high school. The crack in the cliff was bigger and deeper than it had appeared from below, and the chocks I had brought were too small. By the time I climbed about thirty feet above the starting ledge, I was able to secure only one piece of protection, about halfway up. Then came a difficult move. As I tried to maneuver over a bulge in the rock, I keeled over backward and plunged headfirst toward the granite ledge, not knowing if my fall would be arrested by the rope or by the crunch of head meeting rock. The rope caught me when my head was less than two feet from impact.

One of my climbing companions asked, "Well, do you believe in God now?" From the little I had gleaned about his life—I don't think we had ever talked religion—it was obvious that he was joking. But it was no joking matter for me. I realized that when I was falling, *someone* had been present to me. Not some abstract though benevolent consciousness—someone who knew me, who cared about me, who held my life in his hands. But could an intelligent person really believe in a personal God? And what would it cost me if I chose to believe?

I finally found answers through another force of nature, Dr. Matthew Evans, the chairman of the Humanities Department at San Francisco State University. He turned out to be the wisest person I have ever known, and he became my father in the Faith, opening my heart and mind to Christ and his Church. With the professor's guidance, I began to read the Bible and the works of St. Augustine. To the surprise of those who knew me, I became convinced not only that God was real but also that he was drawing me to him. Along with my growing faith, my understanding of sexuality began to change—but slowly. Unfortunately, much of the modern Catholic literature I read and most of the Catholics I knew at the time were influenced as much by the sexual revolution as by the authentic teachings of Christ.

In 1975, I worked at a summer camp for physically and developmentally challenged children and met a lovely young woman who ran the horseback-riding program. I developed a new attraction to horses and persuaded her to give me riding lessons. It turns out that learning how to ride is a lot like learning how to govern our passions so that they can serve love in an appropriate way. The horse, whose name was Vodka, was bigger and stronger than I was. I had to learn how to place a bit in his mouth and use my reason to govern this powerful creature so that he would not take off at full speed, leaving me hanging on to the saddle for dear life. In a similar way, sexual desire can overwhelm reason and plunge us into dodgy situations. The challenge is to learn how to insert the bit of self-discipline and modesty and use the reins of reason and love to guide these powerful animal forces on the paths of true friendship.

The horse-lady kept me on a short rope. She was only interested in a friendship, and so we became friends. I survived my lessons on Vodka, and after the summer was over, we began to exchange letters via good old U.S. mail. She had been a Catholic from birth, and I was in the process of conversion. It's amazing how revealing and romantic letters can be. As time went on, we became better and better friends. In 1976, I asked her if she could be my friend *and* my wife. She decided that she could. I was baptized in 1977, and Patricia and I were married in 1978.

Jesus intervenes

The instructions we received in our marriage preparation program barely touched on sexual teachings except to imply that it was an area ruled by individual conscience. Contraception seemed to us to be a necessity of modern life. We wanted to have a big family, but not yet, especially since I was working for next to nothing in a startup company and we were dependent on Patricia's income from her job as an occupational therapist.

About a year into our marriage, we read Pope Paul VI's encyclical letter *Humanae Vitae*. It rocked our world. To our dismay, it clearly rejected contraception and ruled out using individual conscience as a way to override the teaching of Christ through his Church. The teaching does allow for the use of Natural Family Planning to space pregnancies when there is a serious reason, but we had never heard of NFP. We knew nothing about how it worked or its scientifically proven reliability. We talked and prayed and fretted.

To our surprise, it eventually became evident that Jesus was inviting us to make a leap of faith. He was calling us to trust that he knows what is best for us. Patricia and I finally came to the difficult decision to throw away the contraceptives.

Surprised by beauty

More of the story of our struggles and eventual success will be told later in this book. At this point, suffice it to say that we learned Natural Family Planning, which enables a couple to identify the fertile times in the wife's monthly cycle and to use that knowledge to either seek or postpone pregnancy. It was difficult for us until we discovered the Couple to Couple League, an organization that teaches not only the *how* of Natural Family Planning but also the *why*. Through the Couple to Couple League, we discovered the Theology of the Body teachings of St. John Paul II, which reveal the depths of God's marvelous plan for marriage, sexuality, and family life and are the inspiration for this book.

After switching to NFP, we were still the same ordinary, flawed people, but what emerged was something deeper, a hint of something divine. Although I struggled with the abstinence required to avoid pregnancy during the fertile times, we were both convinced that we had discovered the truth and that the truth had set us free to love each other more profoundly. We decided that we should bring this life-changing truth to others by becoming a volunteer teaching couple for the Couple to Couple League. Over the past thirty years, we have seen this liberating, though sometimes difficult, truth deepen the love and enrich the marriages of the many couples we have taught.

This book has grown out of these experiences, out of Patricia's and my love story, and the stories of many others. It is especially for engaged couples who want to drink from the fountain of love that God has created and are ready to explore the mystery and blessing of marriage—with all its challenges and beauties—as a sacred means to share in creative love. May it inspire and support you as you create your own love story, and help you enrich the love stories of others as well.

INTRODUCTION

Dear Engaged Couples: Sorry for the Fumble!

A FUMBLE CAN BE A DISASTER IN A FOOTBALL GAME. When the player with the ball is hit hard, it's easy to lose control. The chaos of a fumble is of a much greater magnitude when it is the Church that drops the ball—but that is just what has happened in the past fifty years. The Church's team was hit hard by the sexual revolution. While the formal teaching remained on track, the team on the field often lost control of the ball, which represents God's beautiful plan for marriage.

During this disarray, team members scrambled in different directions. Some priests, deacons, and marriage preparation programs downplayed challenging teachings regarding sex and marriage. A much smaller number went in the opposite direction, proclaiming the challenging teachings in isolation, without the full context of beauty and love that illumines their importance and meaning.

More recently, the Church's team has been regaining possession and is moving the ball down the field. In the process, the Church is rediscovering a surprising fact: according to God's design, not only does Christian teaching help couples to understand and live their love in marriage, but also Christian marriages and families bear witness before the whole world—married and single alike—of the power and beauty of the gospel. To put it another way, God purifies our human love with his divine love and then uses our purified love to teach others about the joy of human *and* divine love.

During this time of fumble recovery, couples with a wide variety of backgrounds are attending marriage preparation programs run by Catholic parishes or dioceses. Some have been to youth programs and Theology of the Body websites and are well versed about God's plan for marriage. Others show up without any notion that the Church has been entrusted with a unique insight into marriage. Some engaged and recently married couples have attended Catholic schools and have attended Mass regularly, yet they have never heard an intelligent presentation of the meaning of marriage—especially sacramental marriage, which reflects the love of Jesus for his Bride, the Church, and participates in the life of the Trinity.

Many Catholics arrive at their first marriage preparation class with a vague sense that there are teachings against contraception and sterilization, but they have no idea why. Many know nothing about modern Natural Family Planning. They may have been sexually active for years, and contraceptives may be a habitual part of their lives. It's late in the game to suddenly hand them the football, point out distant goalposts, and wish them luck as the opposing team launches another blitz.

So, first of all, we clergy, parents, teachers, and other Christians responsible for passing on the gospel owe an apology to those of you Catholics who have in effect been denied the opportunity to learn about the authentic teaching of Christ. You had a right to hear this stuff, in an age-appropriate way, beginning before puberty. It is sad and unfortunate that it is sometimes sprung on you for the first time during marriage preparation, when you tend to be preoccupied with thousands of details. This lack of preparation can make it difficult to absorb and accept the challenging truth of God's design for marriage.

It is nevertheless worth whatever effort is necessary to learn and live God's plan. God originated marriage in a way that lifts us into his goodness and glory. He has made us in his own image so that we can become who we are meant to be; but that can happen only when we give ourselves away in love as he does, for the good of another.

Finding a foundation for authentic love
Everyone is called to a life of love, but those who are called to marriage live out this calling in a particular way. If you are involved in this process yourself or are helping others who are, this book is for you.

- Are you a Catholic or engaged to a Catholic, and planning to get married in the Catholic Church?

- Were you and your spouse married outside the Catholic Church and are now considering seeking the grace and blessings of a Catholic marriage (known as convalidation)?

- Are you already married in the Catholic Church and seeking to deepen your understanding of God's intention and plan for marriage?

- Are you a priest, deacon, parish staff member, or lay leader who counsels engaged or married couples or helps with marriage enrichment programs or marriage preparation programs such as Engaged Encounter?

- Are you single and discerning whether you are called to the vocation of marriage, and interested in learning from the faithful witness of married couples?

The good news is that God has a plan for you, and he provides the means for writing your own love story in the context of his love story. This book will help you in that process. If you are marrying a Catholic Christian and are not Christian yourself, *Your Love Story* will do more than help you to understand the beliefs of your spouse; you will find much here about marriage that makes good sense simply based on the careful observation of human nature.

Your Love Story can be used as a primary text for marriage preparation programs or in addition to other materials chosen by the priest, deacon, or other parish staff. You may be asked to read and discuss specific chapters at home to prepare for and add depth to group meetings or individual counseling sessions. Even if the book is not assigned or you are not attending a program, you can read it on your own. And you can grow in knowledge and love by reading and discussing the book long after you have taken your vows, as you strive to live them out amid the surprises and challenges of real life.

Discoveries ahead

For many couples, the decision to get married in the Church hinges on belief in God by at least one of the partners, and also on whether they think the Church offers the understanding and grace to help make their marriage stronger and happier. Although I am most excited about marriage in its fullest development and expression—as a sharing in the work of Christ and a participation in the life of God—I know from many years of working with engaged couples that most readers, Catholic and non-Catholic, will have a more practical focus. In marriage, however, the spiritual and the practical are united. The loftiest love, for example, shows itself in small acts of kindness and forgiveness; and those small acts, day in and day out, are profound expressions of the spirit. So, like matrimony itself, *Your Love Story* weaves together the spiritual and the practical, the heavenly and the earth-ly. It touches on many of the issues that you will inevitably face as you be-gin to write your own love story, and will provide numerous takeoff points for exploration.

We begin our journey together in the first chapter by exploring the nature of complete friendship and hearing the inspiring pre-Christian story of the marriage bed of Odysseus and Penelope. After considering a God-centered vision of love, we will turn in chapter 2 to the practical necessities of good communication, so easy to neglect but vital in the day-to-day life of your marriage. In the next three chapters, we will compare four distinct types of marriage or marriage-like arrangements, including the most complete form: sacramental covenant marriage.

We will then focus on your great "I do!"—the act of consent as a free and total gift of self that is the heart of marriage. This understanding of marriage prepares us to consider the great dance of courtship, in which you will learn how to move through the practical realities of married life to the music of love, without stepping on each other's toes.

The wonder of sex is next, in which the self-giving proper to husband and wife renews their marriage vows, deepens their union, and involves them in God's great work of creation. The fact that fallen human beings must work to raise sexuality from selfish gratification to serve authentic love leads us to a consideration of the challenges and the numerous benefits of Natural Family Planning.

Finally, we return for a deeper look into sacramental covenant marriage to get a glimpse of its unexpected beauty as a fountain of life, a profound friendship, and a sharing in the life of God.

Additional features

To help you explore the many facets of engagement and marriage, at the end of each chapter you will be invited to look more deeply into how some of the insights about life, love, and marriage discussed in that chapter apply to you as a couple. The questions under the heading "Creating Your Love Story" are meant to be both supportive and challenging. They will help you—with the grace that only God's love can provide—to move toward the goal of merging two very different personalities into a union of grace, joyful devotion, and growing maturity.

Six short essays throughout the book reveal moving insights by husbands and wives who have struggled in their marriages and found a deeper faith in the process of writing their own love stories. In addition, two priests reflect on the intersection of marriage and God's love story.

The supplement contains prayers and readings for the wedding ceremony, which you can use in two ways: to select the actual prayers and readings for your wedding, and during your reflection and prayer time with each other.

The annotated resource list at the back of the book offers suggestions for a wide range of marriage resources well worth exploring.

Although the material unfolds with a certain logic, it is fine to jump around to topics of special interest. Spend as much time as you need with each chapter to absorb the concepts, and feel free to add notes, highlight passages you want to return to, and dog-ear pages! The book may be profitably reread many times; you may even want to make it a tradition to read parts of it together every year on your anniversary.

Touchdown!

Even if the Church's team fumbled the ball of God's plan for marriage, writing your own love story will give you the opportunity to recover the fumble and take off together for a touchdown. If you are willing to run for the daylight even in difficult circumstances, you will find that God is running with you, opening the way before you. As you are infused with this blessing, remember that goodness multiplies when it is shared. The Christian team will need your help as quarterbacks, receivers, linebackers, tackles, and kickers—that is, as teachers, bloggers, donors, promoters, witness couples, good neighbors, involved citizens, and wise parents.

Along whatever paths God leads you, you will be called to bear witness to the meaning of marriage. In a society that has become so confused that many people no longer know where the end zone is, you will become a beacon of light, helping to bring order and meaning to your own family and to society as a whole.

CHAPTER ONE

Seeking Your Vision of Love

LOVE. A LITTLE WORD WITH BIG EXPECTATIONS. "Love" means a million things. It can cause exhilaration—and bitter disappointment. It can deceive or reveal. It can hurt or heal.

Marriage. This is a bigger word than *love*—twice as long, in fact. It's not as free-floating or shape-shifting as love. Marriage is commitment. It has an "until death do us part" character. It is love made to grow up and settle down—or die trying.

Happy marriages and happy families don't happen by luck or magic. It's not like in the movies, where all the drama occurs *before* you connect with your soul mate and, once connected, you can just kick back and live happily ever after. In real life, either you make constant and faithful efforts to continue to grow in love, or you slip backward—and perhaps inadvertently slip out of love. But first you need to know what you are trying to achieve in your relationship—*you need a vision of the love and happiness you seek.* This book directs you toward such a vision, and that vision is as much dependent on common sense as it is on religion. So, let's take a first look at the nature of love.

Love as a complete friendship
The vision of happiness starts with friendship—*a great marriage is a great friendship.* The Greek philosopher Aristotle taught that there are three kinds

of friendship: the friendship of advantage, the friendship of pleasure, and complete friendship, or what we might call the friendship of the person. You might, for example, seek the friendship of an important business executive because she could help your career. Another friendship might be based on the shared pleasure in a hobby or a sport. In these legitimate but incomplete kinds of friendship, we mainly seek an advantage or pleasure that comes through or along with our friend.

In complete friendship, however, we love the person for himself or herself. Aristotle said that this kind of friendship, which only works between equals, is rare, and it tends to be permanent because it is focused on the person and not on shifting circumstances. Marriages tend to be happy when the spouses intend not a mere friendship of advantage or of pleasure but rather a friendship of persons, a complete friendship in which each spouse delights, above all, in the good of the other.

Love as a decision
Many people think love is all about emotion—that it is a passionate desire or a very positive feeling about someone. Love becomes sweet magic when you fall for someone and discover that the one you love feels the same about you. The two of you seem to make each other whole. You soar above the rest of the world, which can't comprehend the joy of your love. There is nothing your love cannot do.

Emotion grabs you and focuses you on a particular beloved person. Ultimately, however, love is greater than raw emotion alone. Love involves a freely made choice, a decision to give yourself completely and permanently, and to care for each other no matter what. Love proves its real worth when your emotions may not be all that positive but you choose to love anyway.

Pizza-love or people-love?
I really like sausage pizza. When I am hungry, I love the way it smells, looks, and tastes. But when I am full, I don't love sausage pizza so much. In fact, I don't love sausage pizza at all in the highest sense of the word "love." We have been created to *use* things (including pizza) and *love* people. It is right to use *things* for the good of people, but people are not to be used. I "use" sausage pizza because I think it is good (in moderation) for someone I do love—in this case, myself. When my hunger is satisfied, it's temporarily all over between me and sausage pizza.

It's all right to treat a pizza that way—I've never made one cry. It is not okay to treat a person that way. If I think other people exist to satisfy my needs, I'll be stuck at the level of pizza-love and may never know the joy of people-love.

People-love is harder than pizza-love. It is also much grander. Pizza-love makes me fat (the beer helps). People-love makes me good. Pizza-love is all about me. People-love carries me out of myself in the service of another.[1]

The essence of love
All people are worthy of authentic love—and this applies especially to one's spouse. To really love a person is to give oneself for the good of that person. This type of love involves three things: a lover, a beloved, and a gift exchanged between the two.[2] In Christian marriage, the gift exchanged is threefold: the gift of oneself, the gift of children, and the gift of the Holy Spirit. These three gifts, as we shall see, are closely related.

As the Bible says, God is love. Christians believe that God is three Persons: the Father, who gives himself for the Son; the Son, who gives himself for the Father; and the Holy Spirit, who is the love-gift between the Father and Son. God is thus the very pattern and source of people-love. We humans need help to truly love. Otherwise, our selfishness can clip love's wings and bring us crashing back to earth. For sustained flight, we need help from one who loves us way more than we could ever love one another. God's love is not like our human love. His love has no element of selfishness, and it does not switch off and on. He always loves us, whether we are good or bad, whether we love him or not. It is his nature to love. He is the one who can purify our human love. He can make our people-love strong, deep, and permanent.

Marriage as a vocation of love
According to St. John Paul II's Theology of the Body, love for human beings is not only an act of the soul; it also involves our bodies. *It is the God-given purpose of our lives to make the invisible love of God visible and tangible in our material world.*[3] That's what we are here for. Our maleness and our femaleness are very much a part of both our physical and spiritual existence. Our bodies express our humanity and enable us to make a gift of ourselves to others *in the flesh*, according to God's plan.

We all embark on adult life as single men and women, called to love and serve others with our souls and bodies in ways appropriate to that particular calling. Some men and women discern a vocation to maintain the unmarried state while living in the world, or in the priesthood, or in a consecrated religious life sealed with formal vows. These individuals are not stripped of their sexuality but rather offer to sacrifice its natural physical fulfillment in order to focus all of their creative energy on serving others according to the pattern given by Christ himself. Other people are called to marriage as their way to live out the universal vocation to bear witness to God's love. In matrimony, self-giving love is expressed in many ways, but especially and uniquely in the way a husband and wife's bodies have been designed for mutual self-gift—and all that supports and flows from that self-giving.

God's love is spiritual, but especially because of the miracle of Jesus's incarnation, it is also physical. Marriage bears beautiful witness to the physical, incarnational aspect of God's love. The witness of the priesthood, on the other hand, helps us keep a proper perspective so that we do not become materialistic. The priest, often using physical means, raises our hearts to the spiritual, transcendent character of God's love.

Fr. Joseph Illo, the pastor of Star of the Sea Church in San Francisco and a former chaplain at Thomas Aquinas College, is working to establish a community in San Francisco of Oratorian Priests of St. Philip Neri. Here he reflects on his vocational discernment and what it can teach us about the universal call to a life of love and beauty.

Human beings are physical creatures, so how do I tell a love story that never expresses itself in physical union? Don't we unconsciously assume that a priest's or nun's love is somewhat sterile, even love*less*? Who would be interested in a priest's story of celibate love?

Rather than describing a priest's love as celibate (which comes from a negative Latin word for "unmarried"), I would describe it as virginal. Doesn't everyone want to love a virgin? Don't we all want to give our beloved a pure, virginal love? Jesus said that in heaven there will be no marrying or giving in marriage, presumably because our love will be perfectly virginal, hence not in need of help from a sacrament. Consecrated people aspire to express this purest of love even on earth.

God has called some to consecrated celibacy so as to point married people to the perfection of love, which is completely selfless. In physical intercourse, I suppose, there is always at least some trace of selfishness (in the same way one cannot eat food without at least some trace of concupiscence, or greed). Of course, we who are called to virginity fail most of the time to express that perfect self-gift our virginity signifies. But for what it's worth, here is my story:

In my last two years of college, I dated a beautiful young woman. Several people (including the local vocations director) had asked me to consider the priesthood, but I could not imagine life without a wife and children. Theresa and I loved to attend daily Mass, teach catechism, and read saints' lives together, but I discovered that a girlfriend takes a lot of time. I had to choose whether to direct the love overflowing from my young heart to her or to the Church.

It was traumatic for both of us, but I told her after graduation that I had to seek my path in life elsewhere. I went to Oxford to continue my studies in

English literature. In the local parish choir, I met a young lady with a lovely voice. She invited me to her apartment for coffee and poetry reading. It was all very chaste, and I was still open to marriage.

One bitterly cold and foggy night, I was riding back from university on my bicycle. I came to a juncture in the Woodstock Road. If I turned right, I would arrive at a cheery apartment where a lovely young lady would offer me hot coffee and pastries beside a burning fire, at which we would read beautiful poetry. Turning left, I would arrive at the remains of Godstow Abbey. I liked to pray alone at this abandoned monastery beside the Thames, in whose bare ruined choir stars served for a roof and grassy earth for a floor. It had been dissolved under the Elizabethan persecutions and stood on a broad moor in silent witness to the consecrated women who lived and prayed there since its establishment in 1133.

I turned left, and that has made all the difference. I spent an hour in prayer and then went home to read in my room. On that night, God showed me my heart's longing—to look up through the chapel's stone latticework into the stars rather than through a hearth fire into the eyes of a woman. The choirs of Godstow, empty but resonant with echoes of sung prayer, are my love story. I don't pretend to understand it any more than a married man understands his wife, but I know it's true. To love, to be happy in love, consists in choosing what God wants for us rather than what we think we want for ourselves. St. Paul writes that love consists not in our loving God, but in God loving us. Seek first the will of God, whether that be in solitude or in the arms of a spouse, and you will find love.

Writing your love story

The love stories of people who have enjoyed beautiful marriages can inform and enrich our vision of happiness. Even the tragic stories of lovers who fall victim to various forms of selfishness can serve as a warning about the quicksand that can suck the love out of even the strongest relationships. Above all, the love story of God for each of us can take our human love up into divine love and transport us, through sacrificial love, to the heights of intimate communion.

As you write your own story of love—inscribed on the heart with words and deeds—you will find that it is influenced by family and friends, by the stories of the religious and social communities you belong to, and by the stories told in the entertainment you choose and the larger culture that forms you. Marriage, in a sense, can complete us, bring us to maturity, and make us capable of sacrificial love. That is why the external and internal struggles depicted in so many of the greatest movies, novels, poems, plays, and myths of all time are resolved when the lovers finally marry. As a way of introducing the major themes of this book, let's consider what we can learn from one of the world's greatest love stories.

Odysseus and Penelope: Marriage conforms to our nature— rooted in the earth, reaching up to heaven

The wonder of love, marriage, sex, and children is written into the very being of all people of all times and religions. Some eight hundred years before the birth of Jesus, the Greek poet Homer would travel from city to city, singing his poems. His great epic *The Odyssey* culminates in the reuniting of Odysseus and his wife, Penelope. The reunion revolves around the mystery of their marriage bed. When Odysseus returns home in disguise after decades of warfare and arduous travel, astute Penelope wants to double-check his identity, and especially his commitment to their marriage covenant. She cleverly tests him by suggesting that she could have their marriage bed moved out of their bedroom.

With great skill, Odysseus had fashioned a frame for their marriage bed out of an ancient olive tree rooted deep in the earth. This tree-bed continued to grow in the courtyard of his ancestral palace, and Odysseus built their bridal chamber around it. Now his anguished response to his wife's suggestion confirms that he is in truth her husband—only he would know and cherish the secret of that immovable bed.

This bed is sacred, a holy place where a masculine tree of life makes fruitful the feminine earth. It is a place rooted in the truth of what it means to be human, to be friends, to be equal in dignity, to be life-giving, to be husband and wife.

Fast-forward twenty-eight hundred years and consider your own love story. Wouldn't you love to include this wondrous bed in your wedding registry? You could describe it like this:

One marriage bed, formed from a living olive tree reaching up toward heaven while still rooted deep in the earth, enveloped within a magnificent bridal chamber.

But this is a gift that you and your future spouse, with God's help, must build for yourselves. Your engagement is a time to discover what it will mean to be not only male and female but also husband and wife. Together you begin to form what will become your own sacred marriage bed, your own sacred relationship, rooted in the truth about human nature and the truth about love. As you grow in your ability to love, you will build your home around that bed as a place of safety and intimacy for yourselves and any children that may be entrusted to you by God. Couples who are already married can grow in

their relationship by reflecting on the sacredness of their marriage bed and regularly seeking God's help to make their physical intimacy an authentic expression of spiritual intimacy.

The foundations of real love

Many young couples today have unlimited confidence in the strength of their love. They don't believe they need help from the Church—or even from God—to purify their love or to strengthen their relationship. They think they can do it on their own. Real love, however, is always a participation in God's love. The more we depend on God, the more loving we can be. And God himself *is* the bond of Christian marriage. He holds together, through thick and thin, married couples who trust in him. Our "Yes!" to our spouse is part of our "Yes!" to him, and it flows from his "Yes!" to us.

As fallible and changeable as we are, as self-serving as we can be, with God's help we can accept the self-gift of a spouse and make a gift of ourselves. In receiving another person in love and giving ourselves away in love, we come to truly possess ourselves, to become ourselves, to become the persons God intends us to be. Love—that tricky little word—finds a place to thrive in Christian marriage . . . which leads to family, which leads to the family of God, which includes the Church, which shares in the self-giving love of the Trinity.

Most important for building a lasting marriage is to establish God's kind of friendship and love as the foundation. Jesus told the story of two homes that may have looked pretty much the same from the ground up, but one house did not have a solid foundation; it was built on sand. When a storm came, the rain and the wind swept that home away and thrust the occupants into the fierce tempest. The other house was built on rock. The torrents fell and the storm raged, but the family inside enjoyed a crackling fire in the fireplace, a big bowl of buttered popcorn, and a lively board game. They remained safe and secure.

In order to lay a solid foundation, you often must dig down to reach bedrock. It can be dirty, sweaty work and perhaps not as fun as picking out your favorite dinnerware or sampling the reception menu. But it is much, much more difficult to work on the foundation when the house is already built and you are living in it. The storms will come. They always do. The quality of your foundation will be tested. So pick up your shovels, grab a level, and let's go.

Creating Your Love Story

1. Jesus is the Lord of lords, the King of kings. Yet he declared that he "did not come to be served, but to serve" (Matthew 20:28; Mark 10:45). Discuss what this means to you. To what extent is each of you coming into your marriage in order to serve rather than to be served? What does mutual service look like in your relationship now?

2. How are your visions different from each other's, and how are they alike? Where have your ideas about love come from, and how have they changed over time?

3. How does God factor into your understanding of love? How does love factor into your understanding of God?

CHAPTER TWO

Four Ears: The Essentials of Communication

ISABELLA IS AN ACCOUNTANT. Liam works in sales. She considers herself thrifty and thinks Liam is irresponsible. He thinks she's cheap and that he knows how to enjoy life.

Adrianne's idea of a great vacation involves adventurous travel and lots of friends, new and old. Bryan's idea of a great vacation is quiet time at home with his wife and a big stack of books.

Nathan likes marital sex to be spicy, exotic, and frequent. His bride, Jasmine, likes it pretty much the same way every time, preferably under the covers and in the dark.

Vandi grew up with four sisters, none of whom ever left the toilet seat up. Especially now that she's pregnant, she would really like Blake to put the toilet seat down when he's done. Blake says he will put the seat down for her if she'll put it up for him. The toilet-seat war rages on.

Newsflash! Your future spouse is different from you in many important ways. The man or woman you are about to pledge yourself to with your whole heart has a strong streak of selfishness. *Newsflash!* So do you. And if you think your spouse is selfish, just wait until you have kids. So, what do you do?

Instead of becoming frustrated by the hopeless task of trying to change your future spouse, you can choose to focus on the hope*ful* task of your own spiritual development through the practice of virtue. I've never known a marriage that did not improve when patience, dialogue, compromise, sacrifice, and prayer were intentionally cultivated. There are no laws dictating which spouse should take the initiative to strengthen each of these five virtues and practices in your union for life, but it is always best to start with yourself.

Patience

Many years of marriage may rub some of the rough edges off your spouse, but they will not change his or her basic personality. So either don't marry that person or get prepared for decades of your spouse stubbornly remaining all too human in his or her idiosyncratic way. This calls for patience and a constructive attitude. As much as possible, learn to see your differences in a positive light. Your spouse helps you to experience new dimensions of life and to become a more fully developed personality. My wife, for example, is practical, organized, and focused on getting things done. I am caught up in books and ideas and more inclined to let practical things take care of themselves—or not, as the case may be. Sometimes we irritate each other, but actually we complement each other, especially when we are willing to stretch beyond our comfort zones to accommodate the other.

G. K. Chesterton once said, "An inconvenience is just an adventure misunderstood. An adventure is just an inconvenience properly understood." Practice seeing your future spouse not as an inconvenience but as he or she truly is: a grand adventure. The one you chose to marry is a whole world to explore, and is your unique and irreplaceable partner in the great expedition of life and love.

Compassionate dialogue

Marriage is self-gift. It is self-giving when giving is easy and when it is hard. It is a promise of mutual self-disclosure and encouragement. Fulfilling this promise requires words, lots of them. It also requires ears, all four of them. Not merely ears of the head to let the words in, but also ears of the heart eager to receive those words with understanding and love.

This giving and receiving, this listening and speaking, must form over time an established pattern or habit of communicating with honesty and kindness. Honesty in marriage means not withholding yourself, even your most embarrassing parts, from your spouse. Kindness means accepting your spouse, even his or her difficult features, in a spirit of support and healing. Separated from honesty, kindness can tend toward cowardice and superficiality. Separated from kindness, honesty can become brutal and destructive. Without kindness, honesty isn't even honest, because the truth above all truths is that God is love. *Kindness makes honesty safe, and honesty makes kindness effective for deep healing and love.*

If you start early in your engagement to build habits of truth and kindness, you will soon find that it is almost unbearable to lie or to speak in a purposely hurtful way to each other because you are used to absolute confidence and trust between the two of you. When honesty or kindness is violated, you both are eager to sincerely apologize and take responsibility for restoring unity. Difficulties get dealt with before they fester, and trust allows love to grow.

Even spouses who have cultivated kindness, however, will occasionally strike a spark when anger takes hold, and instantly find themselves in a dialogue of fire. If we have not yet established the habit of self-control, awful things can flame forth from our mouths. We never can take them back and make them unsaid. Every marriage is going to have some conflict, and various couples handle this in different ways. Some couples can mix it up like kung-fu madness and still be good friends through it all. Others never raise their voices but can wound with silence or a glance. Many couples find it useful to agree upon the rules of engagement—that is, what makes a fair fight between friends and lovers. Obviously, this would exclude anything demeaning or nasty.

My wife and I agreed to never go to bed angry. This kept us up pretty late some nights, but it worked well for the relationship. Pope Francis recommended this approach while offering some words of wisdom about "maintaining love and making peace" to a group of engaged couples on Valentine's Day, February 14, 2014.[1]

> We all know that the perfect family does not exist, nor a perfect husband or wife . . . we won't even speak about a perfect mother-in-law. We sinners exist. Jesus, who knows us well, teaches us a secret: don't let a day end without asking forgiveness, without peace returning to our home, to our family. It is normal for husband and wife to quarrel. . . . Perhaps you were mad, perhaps plates flew, but please remember this: never let the sun go down without making peace! Never, never, never! This is a secret, a secret for maintaining love and making peace. Pretty words are not necessary. . . . Sometimes just a simple gesture and . . . peace is made . . . for if you let the day end without making peace, the next day what is inside of you is cold and hardened and it is even more difficult to make peace. Remember: never let the sun go down without making peace! If we learn to say sorry and ask one another for forgiveness, the marriage will last and move forward.

Women often find it easier to talk about personal issues than men do, but marriage is a commitment to intimacy, comfortable or not. For most married couples, regular dialogue doesn't just happen; it takes effort. Almost every morning throughout their long marriage, my parents had a cup of coffee sitting in bed together soon after they woke up. That mostly happy, caffeine-fueled conversation helped them knit together the separate strands of their lives. In the busy rush of life, with multiple deadlines clamoring for attention, remember that your marriage is the most important thing of all, next to God. Wise couples will carve out space and time for dialogue and also establish rituals that support meaningful communications.

And there is always room for further refinement. It's an art to learn the subtleties of how and when your spouse or spouse-to-be prefers you to communicate. It makes life together infinitely smoother if you both develop a clear sense about how to express requests, offer compliments, give feedback or suggestions, convey plans and other day-to-day information, and ask each other questions. Will she feel hurt if you say, "Let's stick with the short version"? Will he flinch when you pressure him to ask for directions? Maybe she hopes you will try to reflect back to her what you think she just said, but your usual response is a mere grunt. Or perhaps you would like her to make decisions quickly, but she often needs to spend more time to think about things.

These or other issues and communication habits might not even be conscious, and your partner may simply need you to speak up about them. You will pick up some of this knowledge about each other just by spending time together, but don't be afraid to ask your partner directly what works for him or her and to share what your needs and preferences are. This will make it easier to rise to the occasion in areas where your differences call for compromise and even for sacrificial love.

Compromise

My advice to Blake is to sue for peace in the toilet seat wars. Many women, especially when pregnant, are easily grossed out by sharing a bathroom with a man whose sense of cleanliness and order may not be up to their standards. Blake could consider the down position of the toilet seat as a tangible signal of recognition that his lovely wife, Vandi, is different, perhaps more refined, than he is. It would be prudent and fruitful to at least concede the bathroom as a realm of feminine ascendancy, a place where, by mutual agreement, she makes the rules. Nor should he forget that she has allowed him to take over most of the garage with nonoperating motor vehicles. That Camaro hot rod you're trying to rebuild is your equivalent of the toilet seat, Blake.

Spouses should always try to understand what's really important to their husband or wife and come up with creative ways to help them obtain not only what they need but also what would simply make them happy. St. Paul tells us to "be subordinate to one another out of reverence for Christ" (Ephesians 5:21). It is always a triumph of the human spirit when you do something for no other reason than that your spouse prefers it. The opposite is to selfishly insist on your way and draw a line in the sand.

Some people think that compromise is a sign of weakness, but what is really immature is competition for the sake of gaining power at the other person's expense. Marriage is never a win/lose proposition. Either everyone wins, or everyone—especially the children—loses. If you must compete, strive to be more generous, more creative, and more self-giving than your spouse.

Sacrifice

While compromise depends on negotiation and respect, sacrifice cuts deeper—and sometimes draws blood. Jesus said, "For whoever wishes to save his life will lose it, but whoever loses his life for my sake will find it" (Matthew 16:25). For you as a married couple, that "losing of one's life" also involves an imitation of the Lord's sacrifice. In extreme circumstances, this could mean literally giving up your life for your spouse. More frequently, sacrifice calls you to give up or let go of things that are very dear or important to you in order to put your spouse first. Career choices or a decision about where to live, for example, might sometimes require sacrifice, not merely compromise. This is the heart of marriage: your spouse is so important that you are willing to share in the sacrifice of Jesus for the sake of your beloved.

To give ourselves for the good of another is a challenge. But love proves itself when we are willing to sacrifice ourselves, especially when the cost is more than what we bargained for. This dying to self, which is a type of Good Friday experience, leads to an Easter morning experience, a union with each other in a new, shared life. Through our sacrifice, we experience a touch of divine joy in this life, and we prepare ourselves and others for the ultimate joy of heaven.

Prayer

The greatest prayer of all, of course, is the public prayer of the Sunday Mass. Attendance on Sundays and major Holy Days ("Holy Days of Obligation") is a duty for Catholics, and it is a blessed thing to form the habit of attending together—and to attend on other days too, when possible. Staying after Mass for at least a few minutes to pray together is difficult when you have young children, but it is a precious gift when you can do it. Other occasions of formal prayer are also full of graces; for example, morning and evening prayer from the *Liturgy of the Hours* is rooted in the practice of the Apostles, who met at regular times in the Temple to pray the psalms. Prayer before the Blessed Sacrament, either exposed or hidden in the Tabernacle, is always powerful.

Each person's relationship with God is deeply personal and hidden, so supporting your spouse's private prayer time should always be a priority.

Your marriage, however, is also deeply personal. Your promise to share yourself with your husband or wife includes spending prayer time together. Opening your spiritual life to your spouse by praying together may be uncharted territory for you, as it is for many couples who find that private prayer feels a lot more comfortable. If you have promised, however, to share yourself with your husband or wife but neglect to invite your spouse into your faith life, then you are holding back and going against your promise. Marriage is a bond of trust that allows a couple to do what they have never done before—entrust each other with what is most personal and sacred. This is easier, of course, for couples who share the same faith tradition and have a similar approach to prayer. But it is perhaps even more important for couples with different backgrounds and experiences. It is best to start to pray together long before you get married. Once you get used to it, it's not hard to do, and it can become a bedrock foundation for your faith as well as a source of deep comfort and support during the hard times.

There are lots of ways to pray.[2] Try a variety of methods, and build on what works for the two of you. Here are six suggestions to begin with. You will find others in the resource list at the back of the book, along with further information about some of the suggestions listed here.

Bible reading: Choose a selection from the Bible and discuss what it means to each of you. Those words contain amazing spiritual power. Talking about Scripture helps you to become more comfortable speaking about spiritual matters with each other and opens up new insights into living a life of faith. This builds trust. You can work your way through one of the Gospels—Matthew, Mark, Luke, or John—or use the readings for Mass each day, which are available from many sources, including the website of the United States Conference of Catholic Bishops.

Prayer lists: Making a list of prayer intentions, and adding to it regularly, helps turn the mind to prayer every day and establishes a habit that will strengthen your resilience when bad things happen. Your prayer list becomes a reference point for the many events and people in your life and community, and it helps teach children to pray. At the end of the day, you can pray for those intentions by saying the Rosary or an Our Father, a prayer you have composed together, or a spontaneous prayer. Both children and adults can enjoy time praying at a family shrine or other designated place within the home, even if it is only a corner table with pictures of Mary and Jesus, and a vase with flowers. We worship with our bodies as well as our souls, so physical objects that evoke our love for the sacred, arranged beautifully in places set aside for that purpose, not only sanctify the home but also strengthen our prayer life.

Divine lightning: It is during your wedding ceremony that divine lightning strikes and your two hearts are fused into one. Energize your shared prayer life with happy anticipation of this moment of union, when by your vows and the grace of God, the implacable logic of arithmetic is overthrown and now $1 + 1 = 1$. After you are married, your prayer life should connect back to your wedding so that you can continue to tap into the grace you received that day. One great way to do this is to exchange your vows again, every day, with the same words or some variation. Thank God and ask him to continue to act in forming, strengthening, and deepening your marriage bond. Even if you only say a brief prayer while standing face-to-face and holding hands, you are once again entrusting your marriage to God.

Prayer on the run: I know of a couple who often pray together as they are driving. If they see people crossing the street who look as though they could use some grace, if they pass an accident on the freeway, if they hear the wailing of an ambulance or police car siren, they pray for those in need and also for whoever will be attending them. Sometimes they simply pray for safety and blessing for everyone on the road that day. Infusing informal, spontaneous prayer into day-to-day occurrences keeps you aware and grateful that you can call on the grace of God anywhere, at any time.

Mealtime prayer: When our kids were living at home, my wife and I made it a priority to gather at the table for dinner almost every night, and our family always prayed before the meal. Now that the kids are out of the house, the two of us still enjoy dinner together, and it remains our most reliable time for shared prayer. You can say a standard form of grace, such as "Bless us, O Lord, and these thy gifts, which we are about to receive from thy bounty, through Christ our Lord. Amen." You can make up your own or choose one from a collection of prayers that you like. Perhaps include some prayers from your prayer list or add a Bible reading, especially if you find it difficult to pray together consistently at other times.

Bedtime prayer: The end of the day is a natural time to turn to the Almighty with thanks for his many blessings and with sorrow for thoughts, words, or deeds that may have offended him. It is lovely to do this together. Perhaps read and discuss the Gospel reading of the day and then review in silence your actions that day. Let God lead you to share with each other one outstanding blessing, or perhaps one fault for which you need forgiveness. Acknowledge anything you need to apologize to each other for. Share how you have experienced each other as a blessing that day. Ask God to bless your marriage as a profound friendship and your lovemaking as a renewal of the total self-giving within your marriage covenant.

Putting prayer into action

Poor St. Thomas the Apostle. Missing in action on Easter Sunday, he was unable to believe the other Apostles about the resurrection of Jesus. He needed tangible proof. Jesus appeared again the next Sunday and directed Thomas to touch his wounds. Thomas touched and believed, worshiping the risen Jesus as Lord and God. Like Thomas, we too at times have been missing in action with regard to our faith. And, as with Thomas, our belief can be revived when we touch our Lord's wounds. One essential way is by helping those who are wounded, whether by sickness, poverty, isolation, prejudice, or unbelief. Prayer naturally overflows into action—actions by which a married couple seek to alleviate the suffering of others and share the blessings that God has bestowed on their relationship. Visiting the sick, counseling the troubled, assisting the needy—there is no lack of troubled folks bearing wounds in their bodies and souls that really are the wounds of Christ. Paradoxically, the more we try to give away the gift of love, the more we receive.

> **P**raise God together.
> **R**eturn to him with thanks.
> **A**sk, and it will be given to you.
> **Y**earn for his forgiveness, healing, and friendship.
> **E**xtend your prayers to the needy, the Church, and the whole world.
> **R**emember the sacraments, especially Confession and the Eucharist.

Fr. Erik Pohlmeier, a board member of the Couple to Couple League whose brother and sister-in-law are a CCL teaching couple, reflects on the power of being "schooled in God's love" while growing up in the family home.

I am the oldest of five children, and I can't remember a time when we didn't pray as a family. By the time I was forming conscious memories, prayer was a natural part of life in our home—whether it was Sunday Mass, mealtime prayers, or the family Rosary. Since love requires communication in some form, I am now well aware that I was learning to speak with God and hear his voice from a mother and father schooled in God's love.

God's love was also communicated in actions. My parents' example of self-giving extended to the needs of others, and the life of charity was instilled in us as well. Whether that meant teaching Sunday school classes or visiting nursing homes, it was made clear that we shouldn't become self-absorbed.

My mother and father were also involved in Marriage Encounter and Cursillo,[3] and the community of love they formed had its impact on me when my father was injured in a construction accident. Support quickly arrived in the form of paid hospital bills and help with work, and I understood the bonds of love in action.

Since love works for the good of another, I eventually came to appreciate discipline as a form of love. I needed help to see the error of selfishness . . . and I can tell you that my parents made no idle threats. After losing toys and having to walk home several times, I began to realize that the expectations were high. In the end, I was grateful for the lessons that some things have to be done without excuses, that what I want isn't always what comes first, and that joy really is found in seeing and working for the needs of another.

While the expectations were high, they were always realistic. Sometimes failure is a part of life and sometimes forgiveness is necessary. Both are part of the love that shaped my family. I remember losing a track meet I was expected to win. My coaches were angry that I'd lost points for the team, and I was sure I had let everyone down. As I saw my dad walking toward me, I dreaded the conversation that was about to take place. Clearly, I hadn't yet understood his love. When he reminded me it wasn't the end of the world, and said he was still proud of me, I learned that love is not superficial.

St. Thérèse of Lisieux said that her vocation is love. But that applies to all who claim to follow Christ, because God is love. The seeds of love are planted long before we are intellectually able to grasp concepts. I am extremely grateful that my parents understood their vocation in terms of love and were able to grow us in the field of God's grace. And I am proud now to see those seeds bear fruit in concrete ways. In addition to my vocation to the priesthood, my siblings engaged in years of mission work and then took jobs in Catholic ministries, newspapers, and schools. As they have each married and given birth to children, I am blessed to witness the shaping and growing of new families in God's love.

God's love calls us to unity. One day, that will be the eternal unity of Heaven. In the meantime, we prepare for, and get a taste of, God's perfect unity in the relationships of love in this world. With deep gratitude for having lived in a home where love was paramount, I pray for the many couples I work with in marriage preparation, that they may also live and share God's divine love in their new families, and that they too will be blessed in passing that love on to future generations.

Creating Your Love Story

1. Can you name three important issues about which the two of you have already discovered a divergence of opinion? For each one, consider how you could take responsibility to keep this issue from becoming a major problem.

2. Can you recall any incident when you and/or your beloved could have shown a better mix of honesty and kindness? If it feels appropriate to revisit the situation, discuss how you might express yourself differently now.

3. Consider the following: What kind of adults do you want your children to be? In what ways is each of you that kind of adult now? What can you do to become more fully the kind of adults you want your children to be?

4. Are you willing to regularly dip your feet together into the ocean of prayer? When and how?

CHAPTER THREE

Natural Covenant Marriage (not sacramental but very real)

AFTER TWO YEARS OF INTENSE SERVICE in the South Pacific, my dad, a World War II naval officer, knew that it would soon be his turn for some rest and relaxation back in the States. But he was bitterly disappointed when orders finally arrived assigning him to an isolated Navy base in Hanford, in the desert in eastern Washington. The scuttlebutt was that not a single unattached female could be found within a two-hundred-mile radius. He managed, however, through stupendous good luck—or divine plan—to encounter a superior officer with the necessary authority who agreed to change his assignment to Seattle. He met my mom on a blind date two days after arriving there, and they were married within a month. He was thirty-six and she was twenty-three. They were married for sixty-one years, until my father died at age ninety-eight.

Although my parents were married in a Presbyterian church, they were not really religious. Neither of them had been baptized, as far as they knew, and neither attended any church regularly. But they did have a real marriage, a natural covenant marriage. As people of integrity, they meant what they said when they promised to be true to each other "through good times and bad; for better or for worse; for richer, for poorer; in sickness and in health—to love and to cherish from this day forward until death do us part." They were prepared to completely give up their familiar, single way of life and be reborn into a new relationship that was by its nature permanent, faithful, and open to children. When asked if they had ever contemplated divorce, my dad would quip, "Divorce, never—murder, often."

They did have differences, sometimes serious ones. Perhaps the greatest challenge they faced was raising my elder brother, who had psychological problems, a seizure disorder, and cerebral palsy. My parents loved him dearly but disagreed about how to discipline him. To their mutual frustration, they were never able to resolve these differences, but they were committed to each other and to providing a secure home for their children. They managed to keep the flame of love burning even in dark times. They had very different personalities and often diverged in their interests and views, but they succeeded in being best friends for life. Although they never used the word "covenant," they were definitely all in with regard to their marriage and family.

Marriage is a covenant, not a contract

Just about every adult in a consumerist society is caught in an avalanche of contracts. Whether implied or explicit, verbal or written, we enter into contracts for our cell phones, cars, apartments, jobs, and other necessities of life. Often ratified with a handshake, a signature, or a click on a screen, contracts are meant to be balanced agreements in which you get full value in return for what you give. If you violate a contract, you will forfeit property or some kind of privilege; the repo man might repossess your car, for example. On the other hand, your obligations usually cease if the other party doesn't perform.

In our materialistic culture, the idea of a covenant is less familiar. A covenant involves not things but persons, and it is not a 50/50 proposition but 100 percent/100 percent. If you violate a covenant, you lose not only property but something more profound as well. You forfeit your integrity—your ability to possess yourself so that you can give yourself to another. When people treat other people like things, signed contracts are all that is necessary to govern their thing-like relationship. But when people treat others as the unique persons they are, then covenants are needed. Covenants are agreements that reflect a life-changing, personal relationship. They have the following five characteristics:

1. They involve a personal agreement.
2. They require dying to an old way of life.
3. They are formed by an oath with witnesses.
4. They are ratified by a specific, agreed-upon action or actions.
5. They give rise to a new, shared life.

Becoming a doctor or a police officer or joining a religious congregation such as the Dominicans or the Franciscans involves a covenant. Another striking example is the process of becoming a United States Marine, which obviously calls for a different quality of commitment than becoming, say, a business executive or an auto mechanic. Basic training is in some sense the death of an old way of life. Becoming a Marine requires a solemn oath, witnessed by family, friends, and God, to defend the Constitution of the United States and the honor of the Marines. This covenant oath is then ratified by honorable action, especially on the battlefield. All of this leads to a rebirth into a new, shared way of life, a brotherhood. The change from recruit to Marine is permanent, even for those who are active for only a single tour of duty. The Marine Corps motto reflects the character of a covenant: *Semper Fidelis*—always faithful. Because of the covenant, and in contrast to a contract, a Marine is a Marine for life, regardless of where he lives or what kind of work he does.

Rightly understood, the commitment of getting married is more like becoming a Marine than a business executive or a mechanic. Marriage is meant to be a life-changing, personal relationship. Engagement is like boot camp, but a happy boot camp with kisses instead of curses. It is nevertheless a crucial time during which you discover what's required for giving up a single, often self-centered, way of living. If you survive this happy boot camp and are prepared for a life of self-giving, you arrive at the central act of the wedding ceremony, which makes a real marriage: an oath in front of witnesses, a solemn promise to give yourself freely, totally, permanently, and fruitfully to your spouse.

The action that seals this covenant is marital intercourse.[1] This intimate, complete, and exclusive giving of your body and your whole person to your spouse testifies to a relationship that is obviously much deeper than a mere contract; it is a covenant involving your very self and the integrity of who you are as a human being. The oath, ratified by sexual intercourse, causes a rebirth into a new life. Your life together is naturally directed toward having a family, but it is still a beautiful communion even if age or other conditions prevent the conception of children. *Semper fidelis*—the spouses are to be always faithful.

This raises the question, of course, of how a couple is to find the strength to be always faithful in a changing world. When our kids were young, we hired a woman to come in once a month to catch us up with the housework—or at least clear a path to the door. This woman was a character, with strong opinions and an iron will. One day, she entered a contest to win a new car. All she had to do was to keep her hand on the car for fifteen minutes longer than any of the other twenty or so contestants. Some of her competitors got bored and gave up after only a few hours. Others dropped like flies during the long night. When morning dawned, our friend was one of only three still in the game. The other two were younger and might have had more physical stamina, but she had decided that this was her car and they could jolly well take their hands off her property. More than twenty-nine hours into the contest, the last of her opponents surrendered and the car was hers.

Natural covenant marriage is much more than a mere endurance test, but it does require a firm decision of the will, a decision to be faithful no matter what. This is never easy. We change, our spouse changes, the world changes. As we shall see, however, when couples invite God into their marriage, God's faithfulness becomes active within that committed partnership. God not only witnesses the marriage covenant but also enters into it, and his perfect faithfulness creates a strong marriage bond.

Four types of marriage

Before we delve into the most complete form of marriage, sacramental covenant marriage, this would be a good time to outline the four different kinds of marriage or marriage-like arrangements, as shown in the chart below. Appreciating the essential differences between these basic forms of marriage will help you understand and choose what is best for you and your spouse.

The Church, following Christ, recognizes sacramental covenant marriage (#1 in the chart) as the valid marriage of two baptized Christians. This is, as we shall see, the fullest development of marriage, and it is touched by divine grace. The Church also recognizes natural covenant marriage (#2), which we discussed at the beginning of this chapter. Natural covenant marriage unites a husband and wife, at least one of whom is not baptized and who may belong to a different religion, or to no religion at all. The parties, however, must intend to live in accordance with the nature of marriage, understood through common sense and confirmed through God's revelation, including the key features of permanence, faithfulness, and openness to children.

In the case of unions that are formally recognized by the government (#3) but do not meet the standards of either natural covenant marriage or sacramental covenant marriage, the Church accepts the legitimacy of children born from these legal unions but teaches that such unions do not live up to God's plan for marriage or fully provide what is good for couples, their children, and society. Entering into such a union, which is not recognized as valid by the Church, is contrary to the responsibilities of the Catholic faithful. The Church is eager to help couples in such marriages. Depending on the circumstances, it may be possible to reconcile the marriage with the form of Catholic matrimony given by Christ, through a simple ceremony called a *convalidation*. Your parish priest can tell you more.

Finally, there is cohabitation (#4), in which a couple shares bed and board without making any formal commitment. Such a union is obviously contrary to Christian belief about the nature and importance of marriage.

Four Types of Marriage or Marriage-Like Arrangements

Sacramental covenant marriage: The valid marriage of a baptized man and a baptized woman.

Natural covenant marriage: The valid marriage of husband and wife, one or both of whom are not baptized but who at least implicitly accept the primary conditions of natural covenant marriage (i.e., permanent, faithful, open to children).

Legal, contractual marriage: Marriage formally recognized by the government, but the spouses do not make a commitment that is permanent, faithful, and open to children, and/or one or both of them have a prior, valid commitment or other impediment to marriage.

Living together: The couple lives like husband and wife without any type of formal marriage, although often with the intention to marry in the future. In some jurisdictions, this may qualify as a "common law" marriage.

In the next chapter, we turn to the most exalted form of marriage, sacramental covenant marriage. Not only is this a covenant between a man and a woman but it also shares in the covenant of God and his people, in the covenant of Jesus and his Church.

Creating Your Love Story

1. What people and life experiences have influenced your view of marriage? How have your perceptions changed as a result?

2. What is the difference between a 50/50 relationship and 100 percent/ 100 percent? How would you characterize your own commitment in those terms?

3. If there were a boot camp for engaged couples, what do you think it should include? What do you and your future spouse need to know about marriage and about each other to prepare well for your life together?

CHAPTER FOUR

Sacramental Covenant Marriage

HOLDING HER HANDS, I LOOK DEEPLY INTO HER GREEN EYES and say, "I, William, take you, Patricia, to be my wife. I promise to be true to you in good times and in bad, through the joy of grandchildren and the challenge of aging parents, through menopause and stiff joints, until death do us part." She says, "I, Patricia, take you, William, to be my husband. I promise to be true to you through good jokes and bad, through tax preparation and vacation planning, through malfunctioning irrigation systems and plumbing emergencies, until death do us part."

Patricia and I have been married for thirty-seven years. We have five sons, three wonderful daughters-in-law, and eight of the cutest grandchildren in the whole world. We have been through a lot. We've even put up wallpaper together, which is a daunting test for any marriage. We've shared the joy of seeing our children do well and have endured the pain of seeing them stumble. We have suffered the misunderstanding and alienation that require a sustained effort in order to appreciate the other's perspective and forgive. And we are still together—in fact, more together than ever. We are best friends.

I have recently been diagnosed with a neurodegenerative condition, Parkinson's disease. I can face the considerable challenges ahead with confidence because my best friend is with me. Our friendship is unshakeable because it is founded on our mutual friendship with the Divine Friend. As we shall see, our covenant with each other is part of our covenant with him. This is the foundational love that not only can survive adversity—it can flourish in it.

Every night, we ask God to strengthen the bond of our marriage as we exchange our wedding vows—with a few additions to the original, and some humor. This reminds us of the importance of our relationship and of the daily attention, prayer, and forgiveness it needs.

Sacramental covenant marriage

In sacramental covenant marriage, our human love is caught up in divine love. The potential greatness of sacramental marriage is so exalted that it is hard to express in words. Most married Christians, in fact, have little idea of the immensity of the mystery in which they are immersed. So let's begin an exploration into this great mystery, approaching sacramental marriage from three different aspects:

1. As a covenant within the greater covenant between God and his people

2. As a sharing in the sacrifice of Jesus for his Bride, the Church

3. As a sharing in the communion of Persons in the Trinity

In order to save the best for last, and to go easy on sacramental theology this early in the book, we will discuss in this chapter the first approach and save the second and third for the last chapter.

A covenant within a covenant

The Bible gives two accounts of the Creation, found in chapters 1 and 2 of the book of Genesis. The first story is simple and majestic:

Then God said: Let us make human beings in our image, after our likeness. Let them have dominion over the fish of the sea, the birds of the air, the tame animals, all the wild animals, and all the creatures that crawl on the earth.

God created mankind in his image;
in the image of God he created them;
male and female he created them.

God blessed them and God said to them: Be fertile and multiply; fill the earth and subdue it. Have dominion over the fish of the sea, the birds of the air, and all the living things that crawl on the earth.
(Genesis 1:26–28)

According to St. John Paul II, this first account of Creation comes *from God's perspective*. It mysteriously implies that our maleness or femaleness reflects the profound truth that we are made in God's image, even though God is pure spirit and doesn't have a body. It is the vocation of humans to share God's self-giving love and to give this spiritual love physical expression in the material world, especially through the sexual expression proper to husband and wife.

The second and more primitive Creation account (Genesis 2:4–25) describes how God forms the human body from the dust of the earth and then brings Adam to life with what in Hebrew is called *ruakh*, the very breath and spirit of God. Then this first human being begins to discover through his own experience what it means to be composed of earth and spirit, of body and soul. When God tells Adam not to eat of the fruit of the tree of the knowledge of good and evil, Adam discovers that he has a *will* and that he has been given the power of free choice. He can choose to separate himself from God in disobedience, which will lead to death, or he can choose to give himself in obedience to God, which opens the way to the deeper freedom of life and love. Adam also discovers, by naming the various animals, that he has an *intellect* that enables him to distinguish one creature from another by comparing their natures. His will and his intellect reflect the wondrous way in which he has been made in the image of God. He has been made to know and to love.

To love and be loved by an equal

Something, however, is still incomplete. As God says, "It is not good for the man to be alone" (Genesis 2:18a). God is a community of love among equals— Father, Son, and Holy Spirit. To properly reflect the image of God, Adam must also give himself to an equal. He needs someone to whom he can give his whole heart and whose heart he can receive in return. This beloved must have a body in which the soul is expressed, just as Adam's soul is expressed through his body. The creation of the animals does not produce a suitable companion for this solitary child of God, because although the animals have bodies, they do not have the same spirit, a human spirit. So God casts Adam into a deep sleep, which is symbolic of dying to an old, single way of life. He opens Adam's side, removes a rib, and forms it into Eve. God then presents her, body and soul, to Adam, and the two become one flesh. In the process, they each become fully human, made in the image of God, who is self-giving love.

This original marriage is a *covenant within a covenant*. This covenant between the first married couple, made within the fundamental covenant between all humans and God, is formed by a covenant oath. Like a father presenting his beloved daughter to her husband at their wedding, God presents

Eve. She has already been described as a "helper" for Adam, using the same word often used in the Hebrew Scriptures to describe God as man's helper. Adam then makes a covenant promise on behalf of all humans, male and female. He pledges to God and to Eve, the first wife and mother, that husbands and wives will always treat their spouse not like one of the animals but as their own flesh and blood. Adam and Eve promise to relate to each other as fellow inheritors of God's ruakh, as persons always worthy of self-sacrificing love.

This new, shared way of life is consummated by the full self-giving of marital intercourse, for the two are not only naked, but they are also married and completely in love, and therefore have no reason to be ashamed. This covenant bears fruit when their mutual love brings forth new life—the conception, birth, and education of children, creatures who are fellow recipients of God's ruakh.

The second Creation account also reveals the essential vocation of all humans, married or single, which was mentioned earlier: we have been made with bodies and souls because *it is our job to make the invisible love of God visible and tangible in this material world.* Our bodies have been made male and female to reflect the truth that we are made for self-giving in love and that this self-gift is life-giving. St. John Paul II calls this the "nuptial meaning of the body."

Rebellion

The freedom that allows us to donate ourselves in love, however, also makes it possible for us to withhold ourselves in pride. Our first parents were blessed with God's friendship and by their mutual love. Yet they were still susceptible to the voice of deception, which suggested that the God of all goodness was holding out on them. This evil voice claimed that God was cheating them, withholding what they deserved and had a right to. If they turned away from God, the deceiver insinuated, they would become like little gods themselves, able to determine good and evil on their own.

Now, this is very tempting. If I can convince myself that what I like is good and what I dislike is bad, then I can do whatever I want without being troubled by my conscience. This, of course, turns out to be a fraud. God alone is the source of truth, goodness, and beauty. When we turn away from this source, then truth, goodness, and beauty dry up and life becomes dark, burdensome, and ugly.

When our first parents broke their covenant with God and each other, they not only hurt themselves, but also somehow damaged the human nature passed on to us. As a result, we come into the world with a deep desire for God and a competing inclination to seek freedom and happiness not in communion with God but in the illusory wasteland of independence from him.

God's promise of salvation

From the time of Adam and Eve to the present day, God has never abandoned his covenant with his human creatures, even when we have been ignorant of his goodness, ungrateful for his loving care, or downright rebellious. Instead, like an extraordinarily patient and faithful fiancé, he promises again and again to cleanse and restore his people. He pledged that he would marry his people as a bridegroom marries his bride. God also promised that, in the fullness of time, he would send a Savior to consummate this covenant and to bring us to the shared life of the wedding feast of heaven.

Jesus is that Savior. He is the Divine Bridegroom who, out of love for us, took upon himself the eternal consequences of our rebellion against God. On the Cross, he entered into our alienation from God the Father and from one another, so that he could share with us the eternal joy of his unity with the Father.

Effects of the Fall

The first step in receiving the grace that Jesus has won for us through his sacrifice on the Cross is to recognize the devastating consequences of the rebellion of our first parents—and of our own rebellion. When Adam and Eve rebelled against God, not only did they fight with each other, but as St. Augustine and others have observed, their bodies rebelled against their souls. Turning away from God resulted in the loss of unity and integrity. Their passions became uncontrolled, threatening their identity and freedom and leading them into misdeeds they didn't want to commit.

We have been made for love, but how can we love when we are entangled in deceit, fear, greed, pride, anger, or lust? God's awesome plan for marriage is still imprinted in our bodies and our hearts even after this devastating fall, but the innocent and honest friendship that enabled our first parents to live out that plan has been trampled underfoot, and we find ourselves inclined to selfishness, domination, and manipulation.

The rebellion of Adam and Eve, still at work in us—their descendants—has also damaged our relationship with God. In the good old days of Paradise, the original human couple would stroll around the Garden, conversing with God as best friends. They sacrificed this friendship for the illusion of power and passing pleasure. They still had deep within them—as all human beings do—the desire for completeness that can be fulfilled only in God, for whom we have been made. But an honest return to God requires repentance, humility, and sacrifice. In our fallen state, we are more inclined to hide our deep desire for God even from ourselves. The yearning for God never goes away. But it can quickly be diverted into an intensified desire for possessions, pleasure, and power. We absurdly seek in food, drugs, prestige, money, or sex the happiness we can find only in God.

Of all earthly desires, sexual desire is most closely tied to love, so repressed love for God can be most easily distorted into an irrational or excessive sexual desire. In the light of Christian revelation, we recognize that marital sex is full of meaning and beauty that should be fully appreciated and enjoyed. But we also have a tendency to seek more in sex than it can provide. St. John Paul II described sexual desire as "insatiable" for this reason. This means that, while sex within marriage has been designed to be spiritually exalting, married Christians still must practice the often forgotten virtue of chastity, which places sexuality at the service of authentic love.

Chastity for married couples doesn't mean avoiding sex but rather everything that degrades sex—everything that is selfish or manipulative or that treats one's spouse as a thing and not as a child of God. To achieve the self-mastery of chastity, we need the healing grace received through the sacraments, which helps us develop the moral virtues called prudence, justice, fortitude, and temperance. It is only through this discipline that the full beauty of marital sex blossoms.

Sacramental marriage after the Fall

As discussed above, God designed marriage to be a covenant within a covenant. Sacramental marriage is a covenant between a husband and wife that is made within the context of each person's covenant with God, in and through Jesus. This covenant is formed when we are baptized and is renewed and deepened in all of the sacraments, especially the Eucharist. Through our baptismal covenant with Jesus, we receive his grace, which is defined by the *Catechism of the Catholic Church* as "the free and undeserved help that God gives us to respond to his call to become children of God, adoptive sons, partakers of the divine nature and of eternal life" (*CCC* 1996). This help enables us to treat other people as persons deserving of our sacrificial love. When married love is touched by the grace of divine love, it becomes an example of Christ's total, self-giving love made visible in the flesh.

The best model of this love—of peacefulness, mutual sacrificial service, and faith in the midst of the most trying circumstances—is, of course, the Holy Family. In order to expand our capacity for complete self-giving, we need to work at developing the virtues they exemplify. As we grow in virtue, we are better able to recognize and cooperate with God's grace and to love our spouse and children unconditionally. Jesus, Mary, and Joseph are always there to guide us in this process. Their example and constant intercession have inspired and strengthened families around the world for millennia. And as we shall see in the final chapter of this book, God's grace helps us, especially through the sacraments, to share in the two greatest mysteries in all of reality: his sacrifice on the Cross and the communion of Persons in the Trinity.

Michelle and Jeff Chardos discovered that blessings can come to us disguised as hardships. But when we trust in God and accommodate ourselves to his will, we can discover happiness in and through the very hardship we dreaded. As Jesus said to his Father, ". . . still, not my will but yours be done" (Luke 22:42). When we give ourselves over to God's will, our families also become holy families.

"A three-ply cord is not easily broken" (Ecclesiastes 4:12). This Bible verse was the keystone reading at our wedding and became a motto for our marriage. The idea that God and the two of us together could do anything became our rallying call. We even incorporated the verse into our e-mail address. It wasn't until ten years into our marriage that my husband and I saw just how strong a three-ply cord can be.

We had three delightful young children—two boys and a girl. Our boys were best friends, and our little girl was quickly learning how to play football with her big brothers. After much prayer, we felt called to add to our family. We prayed for God's will for the gender of our baby, but we felt a strong desire to have another girl so our daughter could have a bond like the boys had.

When we became pregnant again, we counted the days until the ultrasound that would reveal the gender of the baby. We brought the kids with us to the appointment, and all of us cheered when we learned it was indeed another girl. We basked in that bliss for less than five minutes before the tech called for help. After prodding and poking in silence, they told us there was a problem with the baby's heart; I would need to see a specialist.

I had a history of postpartum depression but generally felt great during my pregnancies. As we waited for the date of our appointment with the specialist to arrive, however, I began to feel that I was an unraveling cord.

I was lying on the ultrasound table at the fetal clinic when the diagnosis was announced: our girl had Down syndrome. Now my rope was down to only fibers. The plan was to have the perfect companion for our daughter. They were going to have tea parties. Extra chromosomes and heart defects were not part of that vision.

Sitting in a pizza restaurant after the appointment, I stared out the window, speechless. In the weeks that followed, I poured out my soul in therapy sessions. I talked for hours on the phone to friends. I spent extra time in church. Seeing my visibly swollen eyes one morning in Adoration prompted a woman to bring an entire meatloaf dinner to our house later that day.

During a very candid conversation with my husband one day, I admitted I hated the loss of control. "I want my life to be predictable." . . . "I can't stand not knowing the future." . . . "What about our vacations when the kids are grown?" These all seemed like urgent issues needing immediate attention. My wise helpmate gently said, "Maybe it's time you stopped trying to 'unwill' this from happening."

I realized then that I had only been concerned with how much I wanted to change the situation, not with how we were going to get through it. During the good times in our marriage, I never thought much about our wedding verse. Now, more than ever, it was impossible to miss the analogy of a rope. When I needed it most, the mate God had chosen for me became that sturdy rope for me to grab on to, for now I was only a pile of shreds.

Eleanor Louise was born on a sunny spring morning. She was placed face down on my stomach, and I held her and stroked her back. I found myself pondering another part of our wedding—the vow to remain committed "in good times and in bad"—and I promised Ellie I would love her unconditionally.

I had some normal adjustments to make to the initial diagnosis, but that period of adapting was cut short when Ellie was plunged into a serious medical crisis. In those first few months, we thought many times we would lose her. Once again that mighty cord pulled us along. The same principle that holds together suspension bridges and pulls barges down rivers pulled me, and our whole family, through this stormy season.

Remarkably, Ellie is now a healthy, smiling two-year-old starting to take her first steps. Our girls have tea parties together, and I have to drag her away from the other kids when it's time for her nap.

A priest who knew of my early despair about Ellie having Down syndrome shared this with me: "Just love her like God loves her." I have Ellie to thank for lessons about doing God's will and loving unconditionally. And I have the sacrament of marriage to thank for teaching me the wonders of a three-ply cord.

Jesus made Christian marriage a sacrament so that married couples could help each other share in the joy of his self-gift to his people and could bear witness before the whole world to God's faithful love by the example of their covenant love. But we must leave for the moment the beauty of sacramental covenant marriage to consider another reality. In the next chapter, we will look at other forms of union that are popular because they seem more pragmatic and less demanding but do not fully conform to the requirements of authentic love.

Creating Your Love Story

1. What does it mean to you that your love story exists within God's love story, and that God's love story seeks expression within your love story?

2. Sacramental marriage invites God into the very heart of your life and your union. Discuss with your partner what this means to you now and what it might mean in the future.

3. The Holy Family—Jesus, Mary, and Joseph—is the perfect model of sacramental marriage and peaceful family life. What can you learn from them, and what can you do to open yourselves to their influence?

CHAPTER FIVE

Living Together, Banana Milkshakes, and Legal Marriage

LINDSAY AND RICHARD MET WHEN THEY BOTH arrived late for a party. All of the cashew chicken and sweet-and-sour pork had been gobbled up. The only thing left was a single fortune cookie. Richard proposed that they share the cookie—and maybe the fortune. He broke it open, pulled out the strip of paper, and asked her to read it. It said, "Your love life will heat up." She blushed. He fell for her hard.

He loved her red hair and sense of humor. She loved his perceptiveness and zest for life. They became sexually active and deeply attached. When Richard's roommate decided to move out, it seemed like the perfect time for Lindsay to move in. They talked about marriage. Richard was open but wanted to go slowly. His parents were divorced and he did not want to ever endure such a painful experience. It would be best, he thought, to get to know each other really well before taking the big step.

As they continued their relationship, their friends became more excited for them. The two seemed made for each other. And they did take an authentic, deep delight in each other. But there was trouble in paradise. For one thing, Richard insisted that Lindsay go on the Pill. He hated using a condom and was wary of the risk of pregnancy—especially because she had stated that she would never get an abortion under any circumstances. Lindsay described herself as an "eco-freak." She composted and recycled; she campaigned against pesticides, greenhouse gases, and other toxins that pollute mother earth. Not surprisingly, she disliked the idea of polluting her own body with artificial hormones. But when Richard kept bringing up the subject, Lindsay got nervous; he seemed to be distancing himself. Against her better judgment, she convinced herself that she would be better off swallowing the hormones than parting with her boyfriend.

Richard and Lindsay provide an example of a potentially destructive tendency in relationships with limited commitment: the person with the lesser commitment can gain control of the relationship, even without trying. The partner with the greater commitment—more often than not, the woman—feels pressure to preserve the relationship and gives in. The guy, perhaps without realizing it, may dominate. The fact is that if she doesn't go along with his way of doing things, he could split—and she may not be willing to take the risk of losing the relationship by defending her rights beyond a certain point. *The more committed person can be manipulated by the very fact of having the greater commitment.*

Premarital sexual intimacy may trigger a cycle of insecurity in another way. Men are often able to mentally divorce reproductive intimacy from babies—the sex/diaper disconnection, as one wit put it. Women are more connected with reality in this regard. A woman's monthly cycles remind her of the inherently reproductive character of sexual activity. Aware of the possibility of pregnancy, a sexually active woman naturally desires a safe, secure place for herself and her child, should one be conceived. A woman in a real, committed marriage can safely and blissfully relax in that security. Her husband has solemnly vowed to be there through thick and thin. But an engaged couple has not made that irrevocable, public pledge. The woman may, quite accurately, feel at risk and seek a greater and more frequent show of emotional commitment than may be natural for the man. He often experiences this as clinginess and is inclined to pull away, elevating the woman's sense of insecurity and creating a destructive cycle. This increases the likelihood of future discord or a painful breakup. A fiancé who is willing to control his strong sexual desires out of respect for his future wife develops the self-control necessary for a lifetime of self-sacrificing love.

Love and responsibility

The female body is remarkably complex. Misusing it can have serious consequences. A woman's body, for example, naturally produces the bonding hormone, oxytocin, released especially during sexual intimacy and breastfeeding. It is good for a wife and mother to bond with her husband and baby, but premarital sex promotes bonding with a man *before* marriage, which can interfere with the clear perception of one's fiancé. A similar confusion can be caused by the synthetic hormones in hormonal forms of birth control, which can change a woman's preferences in men. This can lead a woman to marry someone she might find much less attractive if she stopped taking those hormones. Selecting a marriage partner is one of life's most important decisions and should not be made under the befuddling influence of artificial hormones.[1]

Premarital sexual intimacy can also harden hearts with regard to having children. When an engaged couple indulges in the pleasures associated with reproduction at a time when conception would upset their plans, they may come to act as if children—their own children—would be invaders, to be repelled at all costs. They guard against conceiving a child via masturbatory practices or condoms and diaphragms; they booby-trap the uterus with an IUD; they engage in chemical warfare with spermicides; they wage biological warfare with artificial hormones in pills, patches, or shots. When the time comes to do the parental thing, they may find to their dismay that their fertility has been compromised by the effects of contraceptives and advancing age. It may have also been emotionally and spiritually compromised. If a couple has a habit of rigorously excluding children while seeking their own pleasure, it may not be so easy to switch to "parental mode" and start sacrificing their own pleasure in order to welcome children.

When St. John Paul II was still Bishop Karol Wojtyla, he wrote a book about married love called *Love and Responsibility*.[2] Women and men, he explained, have a natural, physical attraction to each other and a deep emotional one as well. Physical attraction, which is often stronger for men than for women, focuses on the sexual characteristics and overall physical appearance of the body. Emotional attraction, often more powerful for women than for men, is a function of the whole person, and especially of the mysterious ways in which femininity is completed in masculinity, and masculinity in femininity. Physical attraction and emotional attraction are good—they form the necessary "raw materials" of married love, helping to draw a couple toward the union of real marriage. The problem is that we need patience to turn raw materials into a finished product.

When I was a child, I would eat raw cookie dough until I felt sick unless my mom fended me off and made me wait until the dough was baked. It is tempting for couples to gorge themselves on the raw materials of love instead of developing the fullness of love. Rather than teaching wisdom and self-control, our instant-gratification culture encourages lovers to skip the necessary foundational work of engagement, pushing them into the pleasures that God designed for marriage. In a major turnaround from my parents' generation, society now *expects* engaged couples to live together or at least to be sexually active. Couples who choose to first invest in building a proper foundation and solid commitment to their relationship before living together are the ones who must be prepared to justify their now-counter-cultural choices.

Physical and emotional attractions can direct our attention toward another person, but only authentic love can carry us beyond ourselves. In chapter 7, we will look at some ways to move from the raw material toward real love. Now let's consider marriages that are recognized by the government but do not fully respect the dignity of each human person, made in God's image.

Banana milkshakes and legal, contractual marriage

I have worked in the California wine business for many years and have observed celebrity weddings in the magnificent Napa Valley. They are spectacular affairs. The gorgeous bride is draped in a designer wedding gown that radiates femininity. The groom is powerful and rich. He smokes awesome cigars. Ferraris, Bugattis, and Hummers exude testosterone in the winery parking lot. The champagne bubbles over and the music enthralls. The couple has composed their own unique vows. Often funny and poetic, these vows are the crux of the ceremony.

Jennifer Aniston, for example, promised Brad Pitt that she would make his favorite banana milkshakes every day. And Brad promised Jennifer that he would split the difference with her when it came to setting the thermostat level in their various mansions. Shaquille O'Neal promised his bride that he would be true "for richer or for richer." Then the dazzling couple kisses as the photographers and videographers continue to document every detail. A famous chef serves a feast accompanied by rare wines. It all has a beautiful, fairy-tale quality—and a hope of living happily ever after.

Unfortunately, these fairy tales all too often end unhappily for the spouses, their children, and those who are in their circle of influence. The celebrity couple has the joy of fame and power, of money and sexual attraction. They are infatuated with each other—and perhaps with themselves. They achieve a perfectly legal, contractual marriage, officially noted and duly certified by the state. Ultimately, however, the foundation of their union may not be much more than pleasure and advantage. The husband uses the wife to burnish his image and for sensual excitement and jolly times. That seems okay because the wife uses the husband for the sake of enhancing her image and pleasure and financial security. As long as both parties get enough of what they want, everything is copacetic, or so it seems. If it doesn't work out, they can always get a divorce. Their children and property will be divided according to the law or the prenuptial agreement. They will each be legally free to enter into new relationships that now seem to offer more advantages.

Ironically, the problem with all of this splendor and abundance is that human beings are made for much, much more than that. We are not mere bundles of desires that can be satisfied by things, and we are not to be treated as objects. We are persons made for self-giving love. A person becomes fully who he or she is meant to be only through the act of giving himself or herself to another and in accepting the self-gift of another. All human beings, whether they are aware of it or not, have a deep need not to be valued as a merely useful and rare commodity but to be loved unconditionally as a unique person.

Authentic love is the opposite of using another person. Authentic love remains constant in spite of changed circumstances. Authentic love recognizes the beloved as irreplaceable, unique. Authentic love requires more than living together. Authentic love requires more than the thing-like contractual relationship of legal marriage; it requires the total commitment of real marriage, of either a sacramental or a natural covenant marriage. Authentic love alone satisfies the heart.

It takes attention and courage to swim against the powerful currents of popular culture, but that is exactly what we are called to do: "Do not conform yourselves to this age but be transformed by the renewal of your mind, that you may discern what is the will of God, what is good and pleasing and perfect" (Romans 12:2).

Creating Your Love Story

1. If someone asked you to explain why the Church encourages couples to reserve the experience of living together for when they are married, would you feel awkward having such a conversation? What would you say?

2. What does freedom mean to you? Do you think that freedom can lead to a deeper commitment? Can commitment lead to a deeper freedom?

3. What does intimacy mean to you? How is intimacy related to sex?

4. Is there something irrevocable about having sex? How is sex different within the irrevocable commitment of marriage? (Not sure? Keep reading.)

CHAPTER SIX

"I Do!"

Your Journey to the Heart of Marriage

MARIA AND CARLOS HAVE BEEN LIVING TOGETHER for three years and haven't poked their heads into a church during that time, except for a couple of family baptisms and a funeral. But Maria's grandmother would have a heart attack if they didn't get married in the Catholic Church—and, as Maria points out, their parish church is lovely. They have no trouble accepting the teaching that their marriage should be permanent, faithful, and open to children. But they wonder about two things. Are they still Catholic enough to qualify for a Catholic wedding? And why all the Catholic rigamarole? Like many minimally Catholic couples, they wonder if it is worth the trouble to get married in the Church.

It can seem that the Church is imposing needless requirements, but these requirements actually are all about making a journey—a journey to the heart of marriage. The heart of marriage is called *consent*. Consent is your mutual choice to accept the other as a person absolutely unique and irreplaceable as your husband or wife and to entrust yourself totally to that spouse. This chapter, and the whole process of engagement, is meant to clarify—and unleash the power of—your consent, your great "Yes!" to each other by which you will become spiritually one.

Maria and Carlos, you can relax. You're still "Catholic enough" even if you have not darkened the doorway of a Catholic church in a long time, provided you were baptized Catholic or were received into the Catholic Church after baptism in another Christian community, and have never publicly re-nounced your membership in the Catholic Church by, for example, formally joining another faith community. If you are Catholic, even by this minimal definition, then you still have the rights of a Catholic, including the right to be married according to the understanding and the forms of the Church.

If you were both Protestant, for example, you could get married in a Prot-estant wedding and achieve—without any particular reference to the Catholic Church—not only a natural covenant marriage but even a sacramental cove-nant marriage. Without the express permission of the Catholic Church, how-ever, a Catholic, even if only loosely attached to the Church, cannot form a valid marriage, natural or sacramental, in the very same non-Catholic setting.

The following two charts map out both the easy path of getting legally married by a justice of the peace or other person (either secular or religious) authorized by the government, and the process of getting married in the Catholic Church. The latter will obviously require considerably more prepa-ration, thought, and time than standing in front of a justice of the peace or a friend with a day license from City Hall. But this investment in prepara-tion has many advantages. Primary among these is a deepening of your un-derstanding of consent, which can help you achieve a unity highly resistant to the forces of division and divorce. If you believe in God, a deeper under-standing of consent helps you to invite him to enter into your relationship, strengthen your bond, and make you sharers in his love for your children and the world at large.

As I mentioned before, it's always easier to build a house on top of sand than to dig down to bedrock and lay a firm foundation. Over the years, how-ever, a firm foundation for your marriage will prove its value many times. The storms will come—they always do. The quality of your foundation will be tested. But a natural covenant marriage is strong because it is built on the rock of truth. A sacramental covenant marriage is even stronger because God forms the spiritual bond between the two of you. You and your family will be glad that you took the time and effort to do what is right and to become the couple and the family that God intends you to be.

Free consent

Movie star Elizabeth Taylor had seven husbands. She was actually married eight times because she liked Richard Burton so much that she married him twice. Mickey Rooney tied her, and Zsa Zsa Gabor beat them both, with nine marriages. The contemporary Hollywood scene is no more encouraging. Pop star Britney Spears, for example, married her childhood friend Jason Alexan-der in Las Vegas after her highly publicized breakup with Justin Timberlake. The marriage lasted fifty-five hours.[1]

Getting Married in the Catholic Church
An Engineer's View

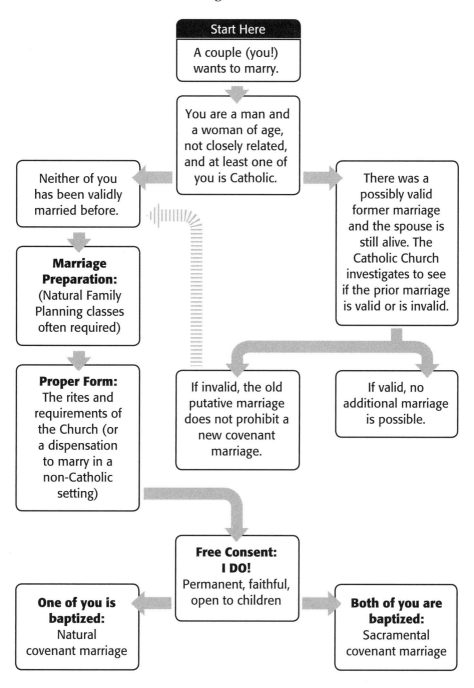

Start Here

A couple (you!) wants to marry.

You are a man and a woman of age, not closely related, and at least one of you is Catholic.

Neither of you has been validly married before.

There was a possibly valid former marriage and the spouse is still alive. The Catholic Church investigates to see if the prior marriage is valid or is invalid.

Marriage Preparation: (Natural Family Planning classes often required)

Proper Form: The rites and requirements of the Church (or a dispensation to marry in a non-Catholic setting)

If invalid, the old putative marriage does not prohibit a new covenant marriage.

If valid, no additional marriage is possible.

Free Consent: I DO! Permanent, faithful, open to children

One of you is baptized: Natural covenant marriage

Both of you are baptized: Sacramental covenant marriage

Getting Married without the Approval of the Catholic Church

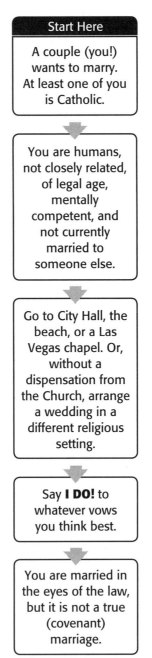

Start Here

A couple (you!) wants to marry. At least one of you is Catholic.

⬇

You are humans, not closely related, of legal age, mentally competent, and not currently married to someone else.

⬇

Go to City Hall, the beach, or a Las Vegas chapel. Or, without a dispensation from the Church, arrange a wedding in a different religious setting.

⬇

Say **I DO!** to whatever vows you think best.

⬇

You are married in the eyes of the law, but it is not a true (covenant) marriage.

How many times do you want to be married? And how long do you want your marriage to last? The chances are that you would like your own love story to be a truly romantic tale of once and forever. But this permanence is not something that just happens—you have to work at it.

Elizabeth Taylor, Mickey Rooney, and Zsa Zsa Gabor all had legal marriages—lots of them. But "once and forever" requires a real, covenant marriage, either natural or sacramental. Real marriage, as we've seen, is founded upon the covenant oath—the freely given consent by which an individual gives himself or herself fully and receives the other's self-gift in return.

Much of the Catholic tradition connected with the covenant oath in your wedding vows can be explained in terms of four conditions that are necessary for consent to be free and three characteristics that ensure that this free gift is total. Free consent means that the couple must

1. *have no prior unbreakable entanglements:* both must be free to marry;

2. *exercise free choice:* the decision to marry must not be forced;

3. *have the capacity to be married:* they must have the mental, emotional, and physical capacity for the free gift of marriage, including the capacity for marital intercourse;

4. *know and consent to the reality of marriage:* they must know and commit to the true meaning of marriage—either natural or sacramental covenant marriage.

If one (or both) of you is Catholic, the priest or deacon who is helping you prepare for marriage will explore these conditions with you so that you can come to a full understanding of their meaning. But let's look at them briefly here to get a sense of how they relate to your personal situation.

Both parties must be free to marry

A number of prior commitments can restrict or exclude the freedom to marry. Obvious examples would include ordination to the priesthood or profession of permanent vows as a monk or a nun. By far the most common problems concerning the freedom to marry have to do with divorce and remarriage. Our society has become very accepting of divorce. The divorce rate is high, and many divorced people wish to remarry. This situation collides—often painfully—with real marriage, which is based on a permanent commitment. Jesus weighs in big-time against divorce, and especially against divorce and remarriage, which he calls adultery:

Some Pharisees approached him, and tested him, saying, "Is it lawful for a man to divorce his wife for any cause whatsoever?" He said in reply, "Have you not read that from the beginning the Creator 'made them male and female' and said, 'For this reason a man shall leave his father and mother and be joined to his wife, and the two shall become one flesh'? So they are no longer two, but one flesh. Therefore, what God has joined together, no human being must separate. . . . I say to you, whoever divorces his wife (unless the marriage is unlawful) and marries another, commits adultery" (Matthew 19:3–6, 9).

Jesus does indicate in this passage one situation in which marriage may be attempted again—when the prior marriage was somehow against God's law. If one or both spouses, for example, had felt coerced into marriage, the Church might determine that the free consent necessary for a valid marriage had been lacking and that the marriage was therefore invalid and would not be an impediment to a subsequent marriage. It is critically important to talk with your pastor immediately if you have been married before. The Church has a procedure for determining if such a marriage was—and therefore still is—valid in the eyes of God. A valid, sacramental marriage, consummated by marital intercourse, cannot be broken by any human action, not even adultery; it can only be dissolved by the death of one of the spouses. A valid non-sacramental or natural marriage is also normally dissolved only by death.[2]

If a marriage was not valid from its very beginning, however, the Church can issue a decree of nullity, often called an *annulment*. A decree of nullity means that a former marriage, even though it may have been recognized by the government and may have produced legitimate children, was not real in the eyes of God, and is therefore not an impediment to attempting marriage again. We will look further into the grounds for an annulment when we discuss the topic of permanence later in this chapter.

The decision to marry must be freely entered into

Real marriage, as we have seen, is all about a free and irrevocable donation of self, initiated before the altar of God in church and consummated in the free self-gift of marital intercourse. This, of course, rules out manipulating, threatening, or otherwise forcing a reluctant individual to marry—it wouldn't be a real marriage, precisely because it was forced. Perhaps the most common problem is when the woman becomes pregnant and either or both parties feel pressure to marry whether they want to or not. Even in difficult circumstances such as this, there must be free choice. Without free choice, there is no valid marriage.

Each party must have the capacity for marriage
Each party must have the mental and emotional ability to make a binding commitment. And both must have the physical ability to consummate—through the unique one-flesh union of wife and husband—the binding commitment they have made.

Offering the total gift of self
To give full consent to the reality of marriage, each party must have an awareness of the seriousness of the commitment as taught by Jesus through his Church. It is not sufficient to enter into marriage as the government defines it or according to private beliefs and preferences. Above all, you must understand that your "I do" is an irrevocable act of self-giving love. This brings us to the three characteristics of total self-gift required for a valid marriage, either natural or sacramental:

Permanent: You must intend your self-gift to be permanent, until death do you part.
"I give myself to you no matter what, even if you fail to reciprocate."

Faithful: You must intend to be sexually exclusive and true to your vow of love.
"I will be true to you sexually and in every other way as well."

Fruitful: You must intend your gift of self in sexual union to be open to children.
"I accept that our self-giving love bears fruit in the service of those in need and may miraculously result in the creation of new human beings, to be welcomed and raised with love."

For each of these characteristics of either natural or sacramental covenant marriage, there is a *minimum required* and a *maximum desired*. It is, of course, a bit strange to talk about minimum requirements for total self-gift: by definition, one expects what is total to be the maximum. None of us, however, is perfect, and a total self-gift requires practice. The minimum requirements describe the starting line, the very least necessary for a valid marriage. No one, however, should settle for the least necessary. All married couples should seek the maximum of love. So consider the minimum required as the ante necessary to get in the game, and the maximum desired as the jackpot of total self-gift.

Permanent

No one wants the pain of divorce. But the intention of permanence required for an authentic natural or sacramental covenant marriage has to be
more than a passive wish; it requires an active commitment, a willingness to
pay the price of permanence. The minimum necessary to create a valid marriage is that both wife and husband, at the time of declaring their wedding
vows, are prepared to make the sacrifices necessary for a permanent union.
The trouble is that many engaged couples are on such an emotional high that
they can hardly imagine the need for sacrifices. As we have seen, however,
married life is full of changes and challenges. And it is just possible that your
spouse may prove to be less than angelic all the time.

As we discussed in chapter 3, there is a significant difference between a
contract and a covenant. If the other party does not live up to the terms of
a contract, you are usually excused from your side of the deal. Not so with a
covenant, in which your wedding vows remain in force even if your spouse
violates his or hers. The fullness of permanence is a human love that shares in
the rock-solid permanence of God's love. God loves unconditionally, not only
when we obey the Ten Commandments, are devoted to prayer, and are generous to the poor, but always and forever, no matter what—even when we have
been in rebellion against him. Paradoxically, the more we love others unconditionally—and this applies especially to one's spouse—the more grounded
we become on the unshakable rock of God's unconditional love for us.

Humans tend to fluctuate between elation and depression. Some people experience these swings more dramatically, but everyone experiences
them to some extent and from time to time. Those who mistake physical and
emotional attraction for the fullness of love may be inclined to bail out when
physical attraction wanes, and emotional attraction can quickly evaporate
when frustration or anger flares up. This makes it tough going for those who
think that marriage is all sweetness and light; but for those who know that
marriage involves sacrifice, it is no great surprise. In fact, it is an opportunity
to prove true to one's wedding promises, which can ultimately lead to joy.

Consider Christie and Dan. He lost his job a few days ago, and she thinks
it's his fault. If he had only shown a little more deference to his boss (who was
admittedly a complete idiot but still his boss). Plus it's been hot, so they hav-
en't been sleeping well, and right now they are both hungry. He feels like she
is punishing him by insisting that they eat dreary leftovers rather than going
to an air-conditioned restaurant with the kids. Feeling as they do now, neither would be prepared to make an irrevocable commitment to the other if
they could go back in time. How wonderful it once was to be single and free!

But no matter what their feelings may be, Dan and Christie are no longer single. They have made a covenant promise—a promise to each other

and to God. To honor that promise, they must exercise self-control and seek the good of the other even when they are hungry, sweaty from the heat, and without income. Although they may not see it now, it is a blessing that their covenant promise, fortified by the grace of God, is holding them together until better times return. With God's help, even their trials can bring them closer together.

Honoring the pledge of permanence takes a strong character even in everyday situations. Forgiveness requires effort, and apologizing when we fail is difficult; but practice makes perfect and is worth all the trouble. The pledge of permanence means that wife and husband can count on each other in good times and bad, creating the security that nurtures children and forms the foundation of a happy family. And that pledge creates a safe space for a deep, authentic love—a love that many people never find but that belongs in your love story.

Beyond these routine challenges are the exceptional conditions. Some couples, through no fault of their own, are thrust into situations of great trial and suffering that put immense strain on their marriage. But the covenant commitment does not have a cancellation clause that can be invoked in order to separate what God has joined together in a valid marriage. If it had such a provision, it would not be a covenant commitment and would not reflect the faithfulness of Jesus, who remained faithful to us all the way to the Cross.

It is true, however, that an innocent spouse legitimately can, in extreme circumstances where physical or psychological danger is present, seek separation—or even civil divorce, if necessary for safety and sanity. Such a decision is serious and normally should be made only when no other course of action is possible after trying every reasonable alternative, and after consulting with a priest and a professional marriage counselor.

But even divorce does not terminate the marriage, as far as God is concerned. If, as mentioned before, a couple has a valid sacramental marriage, and the marriage has been consummated, no remarriage is possible as long as both spouses are alive. This is also true, in most situations, for a natural covenant marriage.[3] According to the challenging teaching of Jesus and his Church, post-wedding bad behavior does not invalidate the covenant of marriage any more than our stubborn sinfulness cancels God's love for us. This is true even in the face of such devastating problems as alcohol or drug dependence, criminal behavior, or adultery.

If there are sufficient grounds, one or both spouses may, as mentioned earlier in this chapter, seek an annulment. An annulment is quite different from a divorce, however. It is a declaration by the Church that even though the marriage was legal, there was a defect in the nature of the original consent between the parties—one that was serious enough to nullify the validity of the marriage from the start. If there is insufficient evidence of a defect at the time when the vows were exchanged, the marriage covenant must be presumed valid and therefore permanent, even if a husband or wife goes seriously astray sometime after the vows.

The permanence inherent in a Catholic marriage is scary. It means that *marriage is a serious vocation.* It requires husband and wife to entrust themselves to God and then to give themselves to each other as absolutely unique and irreplaceable, for better or for worse, until death do you part. That's not a partial commitment; it's the whole enchilada.

Some Christians are called to lay down their lives in witness to the fact that a Christian's relationship to Jesus should be absolutely unbreakable, no matter what. Some spouses are called to a similar sacrificial witness, demonstrating by their own lives that marriage is permanent, reflecting the unbreakable commitment of Jesus to his Church. This level of absolute commitment is hard to understand in our society of minimal, transitory obligations.

Hannah and her husband, who are CCL members, managed to survive a shock to their marriage because of the power of the total commitment pledged in their vows and made possible by God's presence.

> Long ago in a faraway land (or so it feels), I truly believed that my husband and I were going to live a fairytale life. We were both grounded in our faith, studied Theology of the Body together, were planning to use NFP, went to Mass every Sunday, prayed the Rosary . . . the list goes on. As we said our vows, I had no doubt that we would have a better marriage than the couples we knew who lacked a strong commitment to God. I felt very confident that we would live together forever, honoring God every step of the way.
>
> Now don't get me wrong—I knew marriage would be hard. Most people I encountered made sure to tell me so. Yet I never imagined that marriage would be that one hard thing that threw me off my tracks. I did not yet know it would get so painful that leaving seemed like the easier option.
>
> My husband and I slowly drifted apart after the birth of our daughter. We were both balancing work and school responsibilities in the midst of trying to figure out how to be parents. We still took time out for each other and communicated frequently, but we failed to notice that our intimacy was waning and our covenant was suffering. In my naiveté, I always assumed that my husband would be faithful to me and would not let the pressures of lust take him over. I knew he had struggled with pornography in the past, but we were married now and had God in our lives, so what did I have to worry about?
>
> I will never forget the day I woke up to find out that my husband had been unfaithful. I had fully trusted him. Why, God, did you allow this to

happen? How could this be part of my fairytale? What did I do wrong? The questions kept coming, plaguing and haunting me.

For months, I struggled to get through a single day without letting what happened overwhelm me, and for months I failed. No matter how hard I prayed, my emotions and thoughts always won out. For the first time ever, I actually thought that not being married, and raising my daughter alone, would be easier than dealing with the fallibility of my husband's decisions.

But that is what I signed up for, right? My husband was not the only one who had recited during our wedding vows, "For better or for worse . . . " I knew my husband was not perfect when I married him. How could I expect him to be when I am so far from perfection myself? I eventually realized that expecting to have an unfailing husband was simply unrealistic. Although I have never been unfaithful to him, I failed him in other ways—and will continue to fail him for as long as we both shall live.

It has been quite a few months since that dreaded day of discovery. I cannot say that my heart has fully healed, but I can say that my husband and I now have a profound intimacy in our relationship unmatched by anything either one of us has ever experienced. We have learned how to pray with each other and for each other, unselfishly.

I have learned that as a wife, my main role in this marriage is to get my husband to heaven. That means helping him and supporting him through his struggles. I have learned that forgiveness can sometimes be a daily choice but one that makes us stronger. I have learned that my fairytale will never be perfect, but can still be a beautiful love story if only I let God redeem it.

I have come a long way since my days as a proud bride. I feel more real now than ever before. I feel more alive and immersed in God's grace and mercy. I can now see how some people would rather compare marriage to a battlefield than a fairytale. We just have to remember that our spouse is not the enemy—and that God has already won the fight.

Faithful

When you tie the knot in a real marriage, your spouse is making a great act of faith, entrusting himself or herself to you irrevocably and completely. To be faithful is to recognize this great gift and to strive to become worthy of it. As we have seen, the total self-giving of marriage, renewed in marital intercourse, embodies your wedding vows. Fidelity therefore requires that you respect the sacredness of your intimacy, which obviously excludes sexual activity with anyone else, including flirtation. This especially excludes pornography, which conditions its consumers (mostly men) to see the opposite sex as objects to be used for selfish pleasure. We will have more to say in chapter 8 about the dangers of pornography, including its effects on the human brain.

You must avoid other destructive behavior as well, such as the "silent treatment," sarcasm, belittling criticism, or withholding sex to manipulate or punish. Faithfulness to our spouse is related to faithfulness to God: "Whoever is joined to the Lord becomes one spirit with him" (1 Corinthians 6:17). And what we do with our bodies is important. St. Paul writes, "Do you not know that your body is a temple of the Holy Spirit within you, whom you have from God, and that you are not your own? For you have been purchased at a price. Therefore, glorify God in your body" (1 Corinthians 6:19–20).

For a marriage to be valid, the minimum required for faithfulness is that husband and wife intend, and pledge in their wedding vows, that they will be sexually intimate only with each other for the rest of their lives. *But the fullness of faithfulness is much more than this.* To be worthy of the faith that your spouse—and God—has placed in you, you must strive to give yourself completely to your husband or wife. You know, of course, that you will often fail, but in continuing to strive for this goal with ever-greater skill and humility, you discover all the joys and rewards of this glorious endeavor, which will last for the rest of your life.

Imagine that you were offering your beloved a gift of candy as a sign of your love. You wouldn't want to present the sweets in a torn and dirty box with some of the tastiest pieces missing. You would want to give the finest sweets in the most elegant packaging possible. So it is with the gift of ourselves. To *give* ourselves fully to our spouse, we must strive to *become* ourselves fully. This requires us to develop what Aristotle and St. Thomas Aquinas call *virtue.*

Virtue involves the many skills necessary to live a life that is fragrant with truth, beauty, and goodness. If you want to conduct an orchestra so that all the musicians play in delightful harmony, revealing the intent of the composer, you must practice over and over until the music becomes part of you. Similarly, you must practice conducting your life—with its many people, situations, and choices—until doing what is loving and right becomes second nature and your performance echoes the heavenly music of the Composer of life.

The way we treat each other is governed by the moral virtues: prudence, justice, fortitude, and temperance. As explained in the *Catechism of the Catholic Church*, these human virtues are rooted in and given life by the three theological virtues, which are the foundation of all moral activity. The theological virtues—faith, hope, and charity—"are infused by God into the souls of the faithful to make them capable of acting as his children and of meriting eternal life. They are the pledge of the presence and action of the Holy Spirit in the faculties of the human being."[4]

Prudence means that we learn how to consistently make wise, practical judgments about what is truly best under the circumstances. For example, I may prudently determine that I am not strong enough to continue to hang out with a particular friend without developing a habit of drinking too much, and I recognize that the pleasure and other benefits of the friendship are not worth the risk. The virtue of *justice* means that I am alive to the rights and needs of others and that I regularly seek to treat people in a manner consistent with their dignity as children of God. *Fortitude* means that I have practiced and become consistent in doing the right thing, even when it is difficult or unpopular. Finally, *temperance* is the virtue that allows me to enjoy pleasure in its proper context, without it deflecting me from doing what is right, especially when it comes to food, sex, or drink.

Much in our society encourages self-indulgence and opposes growth in virtue. It takes good judgment, discipline, and persistence to keep growing so that we can make a worthy gift of ourselves to both our spouse and our God. To do that, we must constantly lift up our mind. As St. Paul said, "Whatever is true, whatever is honorable, whatever is just, whatever is pure, whatever is lovely, whatever is gracious, if there is any excellence, if there is anything worthy of praise, think about these things" (Philippians 4:8).

Open to children

The poet William Blake said, "A cistern contains; a fountain overflows." God does not intend your marriage to be a cistern, a water-storage reservoir that can soon become stagnant. He intends your married love to be a fountain that overflows with life. Goodness naturally seeks to share itself, and a marriage blessed with love seeks to share that love with others. The conception, birth, rearing, and education of children are the characteristic ways by which the love of a married couple overflows in the service of life. Married couples also seek to serve others, especially those in need, in many ways. As mentioned previously, if a couple is unable to conceive due to age or other physical problems, God will still bless them with fruitfulness in the service of others.

God's council of creation

A comedian once joked about the cosmic negligence of Noah when he failed to squash those two mosquitoes on the ark. As a result, we are still afflicted with their annoying descendants. But what about humans? They can cause a lot more trouble than mosquitoes. Who is responsible for allowing *them* to propagate across the earth?

According to St. John Paul's reading of the first Creation story in Genesis, God "halted" before creating human beings, taking counsel within himself before resolving, "Let us make human beings in our image, after our likeness" (Genesis 1:26). The Bible does not specify what God's deliberations were in this original council. We do know that God is above time and knows the ends of things. He knew that the gifts of reason and choice would be used, for example, to make atomic bombs of terrifying design and to distribute pornography in inventive, cunning ways. He knew of the wars and divorces. He foresaw the blasphemy and greed, the indifference and pride. He had a clear vision, above all, of the agony in a certain garden below the Mount of Olives and of a cross on a hill outside Jerusalem. If anyone ever had serious reasons *not* to make little human images of himself, it was God. No one could blame him if he had refrained. It would be easier than squashing mosquitoes for him to simply withdraw the human race from existence.

Yet God decided in favor of this supreme act of creation. He gave us not only existence but also the ability, through sexual union, to affirm his decision by bestowing existence upon others in cooperation with him. In spite of the Cross—or rather because of the love demonstrated by the Cross—God brings us into being and seeks to share with us his divinity and life-giving power. When married Christians prayerfully and prudently consider whether or not they should actively seek to bring into the world another little person in their own image and likeness, they are, in a way, entering into the creative counsel of God and sharing in the joyful deliberations of the Father, the Son, and the Holy Spirit.

There are always reasons to not have a child. Babies poop and cry and steal your sleep; toddlers whine and need ceaseless supervision; tweens can show a precocious talent for pushing your buttons; teenagers can rebel and sass; college kids may party more than study while burning through piles of cash that could have financed your retirement. Sharing in God's act of creation leads directly to a sharing in the Cross. And yet to share with your spouse and with God in the creation of a human being called to eternal life is no small thing. The only act that is greater is to share in the sacrifice of Jesus for the salvation of others, which is a responsibility of parenthood as well.

Each married couple is called over and over again into God's creative council because the creation and salvation of children are high points of marriage. The intimate union of husband and wife creates a community that reflects the life of the Trinity and is the proper environment for raising children. It is important to reiterate here that if a couple is not blessed with children despite an intense longing, God will open other doors and will lavish great graces on his faithful servants, who will find other ways to serve him. For many couples, this may take the form of adoption—generously opening their hearts to children who need a home, in imitation of our God, who has fully opened his life to us.

In the creative act of making love, a married couple affirms God's decision to create humans, to create them male and female, to help them love, and to give them the privilege of sharing intelligently in God's supreme act of creation. A couple must respect the integrity of God's design, and their union must be open to life even when conception is not their immediate goal. For serious reasons, a couple may, with discernment and prayer, come to a responsible decision to postpone conception by abstaining during periods of fertility. In every case, however, couples must strive to be like God, to remain open to life, to be lovers of life, to be givers of the physical and spiritual life that flows from the self-donation of marital intimacy. The decree of the council of creation is always a yes to love and to life—a yes that *is* love and life.

In creating a valid marriage, the minimum required with regard to openness to children is that a couple not reject the fruitful nature of marriage and sexuality. In other words, couples capable of conceiving children must at least be open to the possibility of children over the course of their marriage. God calls us to responsible parenthood, guided by a preferential option for life. A couple who decides that they do not want children at all are denying something essential to the life-giving love between husband and wife. They are choosing to make their relationship a cistern, not a fountain, and this cannot be reconciled with the total giving that is the hallmark of a natural or sacramental covenant marriage. The maximum desired, on the other hand, involves not only a rejection of sterilization and contraception but also a generosity in the service of life. (See more on sexuality and openness to life in chapters 8 and 9.)

Dan and Carmen Maguire's story tells us something about this fountain of life, which is based on trust and can well up to eternal happiness.

When Dan fell in love with Carmen and asked her to marry him, she had more to think about than whether she returned his affection. They wanted children—Carmen wanted lots of them—but Dan was beginning to have some symptoms of early-stage multiple sclerosis. "But," Carmen recalls, "I couldn't see living my life without him, and I knew in my heart that God would take care of Dan if we trusted in him."

Dan and Carmen were not taught about Natural Family Planning in their Pre-Cana classes, but after doing their own research on NFP and prayerfully considering the Church's teaching on contraception, they knew that God was calling them to be open to life. They had their first child in 1981, a year after they married; their second arrived in 1983; and their third came two years after that. In early 1986, they found out that their fourth was en route.

Dan was now thirty-five and in full swing at his law practice. The MS had flared up a few times, including numbness in his feet and legs and paralysis on one side of his mouth. Because Dan's aunt and sister, both of whom have MS, were confined to wheelchairs by that time, Dan was concerned that if his symptoms progressed to that level, he wouldn't be able to provide for his family. It would be very difficult, if not impossible, to run a law firm and try cases from a wheelchair while dealing with the other problems of advanced MS.

"Back when Dan proposed," Carmen observed, "I had recognized the worst that could happen, and I was game for that. I'd had to trust God when it came to marrying Dan. In the same way, I knew I would need to trust the Lord with my whole life, whatever he chose to give me."

Dan, half joking, told Carmen that he would like a guarantee from God, etched in stone—or at least have someone to sue if things got worse! But Carmen's faith, strengthened by the sacraments and her deep devotional life as a member of Opus Dei, continued to bolster her husband's willingness to use Natural Family Planning for spacing pregnancies. Together, they made a leap of faith by remaining open to more children if God chose to send them, regardless of how Dan's condition might progress.

And God did send them. Their fifth, sixth, seventh, and eighth children were welcomed with open arms, and Carmen became pregnant for the last time when she was forty-five. There were those who let it be known that they thought this pregnancy irresponsible, given the full house and the age-related risks to mother and baby. But by God's grace, child number nine was born whole and healthy, fifteen years after the birth of their first. Two miscarriages followed, and they realized that was God's way of saying that they had fulfilled his plan for growing their family.

In the past thirty years, Dan has had to refinance their home five times to help with colleges expenses, but he remains the proud patriarch of a family of five girls and four boys. Medication has kept his symptoms to a minimum, and most recently, he has taken up playing the guitar.

As Carmen says, "After all, if you believe in God, you need to trust him. If you don't trust him, it means you don't believe in him."

Creating Your Love Story

1. Take a few minutes to review the two charts in this chapter. Are you willing to take the longer road in order to journey to the heart of marriage? If so, why? If not, why not?

2. Consider both the minimum required and the fullness desired for permanence, faithfulness, and openness to children. Where do you stand on the spectrum of each of these qualities of real marriage?

3. The irrevocable commitment of marriage is an act of trust, a leap of faith. If you are not at all scared of that leap, you may not be taking marriage seriously enough. If you are overcome with fear, then you should make doubly sure that both of you are ready for the commitment of permanent, faithful, and fruitful marriage. Are you ready and willing to share your fears and concerns with each other?

4. What is each of you doing to enhance your ability to love by growing in the theological virtues—faith, hope, and love—and in the moral virtues of prudence, justice, fortitude, and temperance? What more could you be doing and supporting your future spouse to do?

CHAPTER SEVEN

The Dance of Courtship

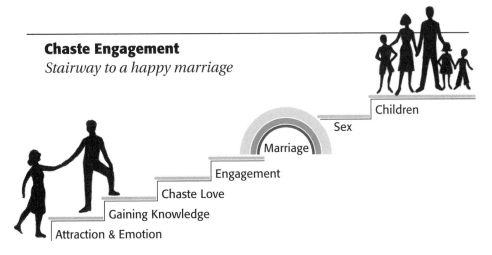

Chaste Engagement
Stairway to a happy marriage

Children

Sex

Marriage

Engagement

Chaste Love

Gaining Knowledge

Attraction & Emotion

AS THE STAIRWAY TO A HAPPY MARRIAGE SHOWS, there is a well-ordered, natural progression from attraction and emotion, through engagement, to marriage and sex and, finally, to children. Contemporary culture has largely overthrown that natural progression, creating confusion and conflict. Now, with the help of the Christian community, you have the opportunity to recover the peacefulness and joy that result from following God's plan.

During his General Audience on May 27, 2015, Pope Francis observed that "the Church, in her wisdom, maintains the distinction between engaged and married couples—they are not the same—precisely in view of the delicate and profound nature of this fact. We are careful not to lightheartedly dismiss this wise teaching, nurtured by the experience of happily married life. The powerful symbols of the body hold the keys to the soul: We cannot treat the bonds of the flesh lightly, without opening up lasting wounds to the spirit," continued the Holy Father, remarking that "today's culture and society have become rather indifferent to the delicate and serious nature of this passage."

He characterized betrothal as "the time in which two people are called to work on love, a shared and profound task," pointing out that "the alliance of love between a man and a woman, an alliance for life, cannot be improvised, and is not made in a day; it is a path on which one learns and refines. . . . It is, I dare say, an artisanal alliance. To make two lives one is almost a miracle of freedom and of the heart, entrusted to faith. We must perhaps work more on this point, as our 'sentimental coordinates' have become a little confused. Those who wish to attain everything immediately, also give up on everything straight away at the first hurdle (or at the first opportunity). . . . Engagement channels the will to preserve something together, something that should never be bought or sold, betrayed or abandoned, however tempting the alternatives may be."

Respecting the natural order of your love story, of course, is not easy. You are powerfully attracted to each other; otherwise, you would not be talking about tying the knot. This attraction tends toward satisfaction through sexual relations. Screens everywhere, big and small, broadcast that *everyone* is doing it. It seems as though almost everybody in real life is doing it. If you are among those couples who have chosen to postpone their sexual union, why should you continue to endure the strains of waiting? If you are among those who have already been sexually active, is there any reason to stop now and wait until you are married? Here are six reasons to consider remaining or becoming abstinent during your engagement.

Six Reasons for Engaged Couples to Save (or Resave) Sexual Intimacy for Marriage

1. Courtship is so romantic! You desire each other but honor and care about each other so much that you are willing to practice self-control. Here is the secret: Desire controlled makes friendship grow deeper in intimacy. This is so good for marriage.

2. What an awesome, mind-blowing, never-to-be-forgotten wedding night! What a giving of self! God's plan is challenging—but oh, the joy! And this will now be the pattern throughout your marriage for all of your self-giving. Talk about "making love"!

3. The exchange of sex belongs to the marriage covenant, as its seal. Outside the covenant, sex is a denial and a contradiction of the covenant. This is not so good for marriage.

4. Sex before marriage usually depends on contraception, which distorts the union designed by God for marriage. Sex becomes using the other person, which damages the capacity for true intimacy and sells the relationship short.

5. A couple who practices loving abstinence during courtship develops a reliance on God and a spiritual strength that can help them remain faithful to each other forever.

6. Our joy and our love of God deepen when we trust in him and obey him, even in situations and ways that are challenging for us.

If a couple who are attracted to each other are able to master their physical and emotional desires, these disciplined desires help create a unique and romantic phase in the relationship called courtship. This discipline allows the growing love they have for each other to become deeply rooted in a growing love of God, which otherwise could easily be forgotten during the exciting time of engagement.

Scripture can be a sustaining help along the way. Try Pope Francis's recommendation to reflect on and repeat to each other the words of the prophet Hosea: "I will espouse you to me forever: I will espouse you in right and in justice, in love and in mercy; I will espouse you to me in fidelity, and you shall know the Lord" (Hosea 2:21–22). The Pope suggests: "May every engaged couple think of this and say to each other, 'I will make you my spouse.' Wait for that moment; it is a moment on a path on which one proceeds slowly, a path of ripening. One must not pass through the different stages too quickly. Ripening takes place in this way, step by step."

Scott Streif, who is a member of CCL with his wife, expresses the beauty of waiting for the right gift . . . at the right time.

I recall a childhood memory about an approaching birthday. My mom came home one evening carrying a large shopping bag. She was a selfless woman and rarely bought anything besides the weekly groceries, so I was certain she had been shopping for my birthday presents.

A few days later, while she was cooking, I snuck into my mom's closet in search of my birthday stash and found the shopping bag tucked in a back corner. I could barely contain my excitement as I peeked inside.

The excitement ended as quickly as it had begun. I knew my mom would be mad if she caught me acting like those gifts already belonged to me, and I was afraid of getting caught.

Unwrapping the presents on my birthday returned some of the initial joy, for I was finally able to play with my new toys. But I also felt an emptiness. Opening each package was now merely a formality, a step to complete the transaction. I kept hoping that my mom had some secret gift I had not yet discovered.

I had robbed myself of the joy of opening a gift at the right time, when it was really given to me; instead, I was left hoping for something bigger and better.

While birthday presents are not nearly as important as saving oneself for marriage, I believe the point is similar. A wedding day offers numerous first-time experiences. Why not also save for this most important day the first-time experience of giving to and receiving each other? Why not create together a memory that will be celebrated each time you make love? Then every intimate encounter will bring to mind the beautiful embrace you first shared on that wedding night and will offer an opportunity to renew your marriage vows.

Trusting God throughout our relationship brought us together to share a truly romantic wedding night. I'll never forget untying the ribbon from my wife's hair, intricately secured like the bow on a package. I recall delicately assisting her out of her stunning wedding gown, ever so gently, as if trying to preserve wrapping paper for the next holiday. The gift revealed was created out of love and passion. I could not have asked for a more perfect gift.

My wife and I both saved ourselves for marriage, and we believe that our chastity is what prepared our marriage for any obstacles we encounter along the way. We sacrificed our short-term desires for the opportunity to share that same desire as a gift on our wedding night. We took a leap of faith in each other, and in God, strengthening our resolve and honoring each other in the process.

The fascinating dance of courtship

So, what do you *do* while you're waiting for the precious moment when you will unwrap the gift and joyfully ratify your wedding vows by marital intercourse? Some engaged couples waste much of the energy of courtship merely entertaining themselves; this will reveal how a person parties and what kinds of movies he or she likes but not much else. More important for establishing a solid basis for lifelong love is sharing real-life situations. Try some of the following ideas, which might spark you to come up with your own as well.

- Go together to visit the aunt in the nursing home.

- Volunteer together for a cause you both care about.

- Take turns teaching each other how to do something that comes easily to you but is more difficult for your partner.

- Sail a boat together. By the time you get back to the dock (hopefully, you do make it back), you will know a lot more about how shared decision-making will play out in your marriage and what your future spouse says and does when cracked in the head by the boom. This is important knowledge because life is pretty well guaranteed to crack you both in the head a few times.

- Babysit together for friends or relatives. If you're really adventurous, include some outings to a public place such as a children's museum or an amusement park.

You will need to learn many things about your future spouse that you can't necessarily discover through shared activities. Honest discussions and explorations will go a long way toward paving the way to marital harmony and can make visible any warning buoys up ahead.

- Take advantage of one of many marriage preparation programs available for couples to examine both shared and divergent interests and values, identify potential areas of conflict, and explore a couple's individual goals and how those might impact the marriage. A bride-to-be should be able to accurately explain her fiancé's views on God, children, finances, extended family relationships, friendships, career choices, home culture, physical health and exercise, and so on. A groom-to-be should be able to do likewise with regard to his fiancée's values, views, and expectations. Each should know what the other believes about creating unity in marriage.

- Incorporate into your adventure of getting to know each other questionnaires such as the FOCCUS© Pre-Marriage Inventory, which can be taken independently and are sometimes incorporated in marriage preparation programs sponsored by parishes. Married couples can take the REFOCCUS© Marriage Enrichment Inventory. (See resource list.)

- Read books and articles that will support you on your engagement journey. The resource list includes several recommendations, including a suggestion from Pope Francis made during his General Audience on May 27, 2015. The Pope mentioned Italian writer Alessandro Manzoni's novel *I promessi sposi* (*The Betrothed*) and invited those present to read it, as it is "an authentic masterpiece which recounts the story of a betrothed couple who suffer greatly, who walk a path full of many difficulties before arriving at the end, at marriage. Do not forget this masterpiece on betrothal . . . read it and you will see beauty and suffering, but also the faithfulness of the betrothed couple."

- Meet each other's parents and siblings and get to know them. Learn how your future spouse relates to his or her own family and to your family, because these interactions are likely to be the pattern for relations in the new family you will build together. You should also be open with each other about any serious difficulties in your families, such as problems with alcohol, drugs, or other addictions; emotional or sexual abuse; anger management; or mental health issues. These topics can be awkward or painful to discuss, and you may need to discern whether to seek help to navigate these waters together.

- Don't ignore what may now seem like unimportant details but are actually expectations that can have a serious impact on your marriage. It will be a lot better to discover now that your husband-to-be expects you to take care of all the food shopping and cooking or to welcome his parents every year for a month-long vacation in the home. Often these assumptions are carried over from your family of origin, and you may not even realize that you have them. My wife's father was an airline pilot with a degree in engineering. If the rain gutters leaked, he would reengineer them to aeronautical standards, so Patricia kind of assumed that this is what husbands and fathers do. I, on the other hand, have learned the difference between a wrench and a pair of pliers, but my handyman skills do not go much beyond driving a nail to hang a picture. The more honest and realistic you can be with each other before the wedding about identifying and negotiating expectations, the easier the transition into married life will be.

- Review together how each of you currently spends a typical weekday, weekend, holiday, and vacation, and gradually get to know each other's habits, needs, hopes, and preferences. Consider what it will take to blend your individual lifestyles to create a home and a life of harmony and understanding. Be realistic. If it will drive you crazy to live with a man who will make you a football widow every season or is a night owl when you can barely keep your eyes open past ten, if you crave peace and quiet and your intended talks not only all day but also in her sleep, you might want to think twice—for the good of both parties. You might heartily agree with each other that the compromise and sacrifice discussed earlier are noble and worthy ideals, but what will happen when these ideals need to be brought down to earth?

Finances: A sticky business

According to poet Edward Lear, when the Owl and the Pussy-cat went to sea in a beautiful pea-green boat, "They took some honey, and plenty of money, / Wrapped up in a five-pound note."[1] Money and marriage has been a sticky business ever since. Courtship is a time to think about what's up ahead, including your future family and how you will provide for them. It is also the time to learn about each other's financial situation, including any debts owed and expected future obligations. In discussing your skills and attitudes, you can discover a lot about your future spouse's generosity, spending habits, tolerance for risk, willingness to postpone gratification in order to save, and ability to make well-considered financial decisions as a team.

Our society is famously materialistic, so it takes awareness and consistent effort to keep financial concerns in their proper place. Married couples must provide for their families and contribute to the good of society and the Church. But we must also always practice a certain detachment in order to keep our hearts free to love each other, to love God, and to be generous to those in need. The engagement period is a great time to study family finances and learn some basics about how to be good stewards of God's financial provision. Even if it's too early to know what your precise financial situation will be when you begin your married life, take advantage of books or courses that can help you learn together how to make and adjust a budget, how to create a financial statement and a spreadsheet for monitoring expenses, and what the basic elements are of a short-term and a long-term financial plan. Discuss your individual strengths and weaknesses in money management, and how you might divide up responsibilities such as paying bills, balancing accounts, and tracking monthly expenses. (See resource list.)

Compare your views on tithing, saving, making investments, managing risk, giving and accepting financial gifts, and borrowing and lending (including from and to friends and family, and from financial institutions). Be honest about your hopes and expectations regarding your future spouse's earning power, before and after any children are born. Consider realistically how much each of you might need to work in order to balance financial needs with parenting requirements. Talk about whether you could be satisfied paying rent (and letting the landlord worry about the leaking roof), or if you have a great desire to own your own home, even if it means spending some weekends doing repairs and maintenance. You will need to keep adjusting all of these factors as you go along, but getting a head start will give you more confidence about your capacity as a couple to navigate the complex domain of finances.

Religious practices
Some couples may discover that they are very compatible when it comes to practical matters but their religious practices and commitments don't match as well. Now is the time to prayerfully explore what you share in common and what your differences are, with the intention of seeing how you might learn and grow from each other's preferences, experiences, and commitments.

- The opportunity to worship together regularly and share your deepest beliefs with each other makes engagement and marriage a fruitful time for spiritual growth. If you are from different faith communities, or one of you is of no particular faith, there will be some major issues to patiently and lovingly resolve. To be married in the Catholic Church, a Catholic spouse marrying a non-Catholic must certify that he or she intends to do everything possible to have the children baptized and to raise them Catholic. The non-Catholic spouse must at least acknowledge that he or she is aware of the Catholic spouse's serious obligation and intention in this regard. Some couples try to raise kids in two religions at the same time, which is a sure road to confusion, or with no religion at all, which deprives the kids of an essential element of human formation. Others may raise the kids Catholic but still expose them to, say, celebrations of Jewish holidays if the other spouse is Jewish, or to some of the rituals and customs of whatever the other religion is in the house. The loyalties here can be deep, and compromise may not always be easy. It is essential that couples discuss these issues in depth long before the knot is tied.

- In addition to how the children will be raised, spouses must make many decisions about their own participation in various religious practices and communities. Consider together your individual tastes, commitments, and desires in your day-to-day religious life. Even if you are both Catholic, there are a lot of religious practices and options to blend. One of you, for example, may love to sing at a local Mass that includes lively, modern songs and a full backup band, and the other may treasure the silent reverence and Gregorian Chant in a Traditional Latin Mass at a parish across town. Are you part of the Charismatic Renewal and currently attending several conferences every year? Do you secretly hope that your spouse-to-be will share the two a.m. Eucharistic Adoration hour you've been faithfully showing up for? Of course, you will continue to discover through and with each other new interests and activities within the Faith once you are married, but the time is now to share openly about what you love and what you hope to do together.

Fasten your seatbelt—turbulence ahead!

Imagine that an engaged friend is asking for your advice. The reception hall has been rented, the cake ordered, the guests invited. For a while, she's had a gnawing sense that the gap might be hard to bridge between her fiancé's casual attitude about planning ahead and making arrangements and her attention to detail. Now she has learned that he never reserved the airplane tickets for their honeymoon as he promised to do. He thought the oversight was no big deal, even when she pointed out that ticket prices had nearly doubled since they made the agreement. What's more, when she calmly expressed her upset that he had not followed through on an important commitment, he gave her "the look" and told her that she gets too tense about things and needs to work on her trust issues. He is a sweet guy in many ways, she tells you, and his happy-go-lucky disposition can be a lot of fun, but she wouldn't be able to live like that. How would you advise her?

Consider honestly whether you would have the courage to break off an engagement, even if it would be embarrassing and upsetting to many people. Could you be kind and yet honest and firm? A person who is not mature enough to end a relationship that is not the right one is probably not mature enough to get married in the first place. If you have doubts about your situation, what wise friend, priest, counselor, or family member could you talk to who could help you distinguish normal jitters from real issues?

Engagement is a time to engage—to cut through the fluff and find what's real. Facing issues squarely requires multiple acts of courage and faith, but each one of these helps you to keep weaving your love story.

Marguerite Bowling and her husband became members of the Couple to Couple League when they took a CCL Natural Family Planning course at their church. Her story shows how a particularly difficult engagement period can make a couple even stronger in their commitment to each other.

> "I think I need to talk with a priest about marriage and learn more what it's really all about . . . because it's not making sense."
>
> I loved my fiancé to pieces, but these were not the words I wanted to hear three months before our wedding date (and one week after the invitations

had been mailed). This declaration by my reluctant fiancé during yet another talk about our future together was more evidence that we had been through a pretty rocky engagement.

My fiancé was, and still is, a wonderful man. He's strong, good-looking, independent, considerate, witty, spiritually minded, and intelligent. But he's also a survivor of a divorced family, which left emotional scars and made him gun-shy when it came to the commitment of marriage.

How gun-shy? When he proposed, he asked if we could keep our new engagement under wraps and just "test it out" between the two of us. Test it out? I wanted to tell every one of my friends and family.

There would be no testing it out, I protested. But I also couldn't deny that my non-Catholic fiancé had fears about what marriage would mean for his life and our relationship. They were valid issues that had to be addressed. So instead of worrying about table placements or wedding colors, our conversations focused mainly on what a potential marriage would be like. We were concerned about what God wanted for us, and several times my fiancé asked priests and other respected authorities (such as our Pre-Cana mentor couple) about the real purpose of marriage. Why did God create marriage? What is the proper role of the husband and wife?

To be honest, it was not fun having to rely on God for answers about our relationship and wondering what the outcome would be. No woman enjoys considering that the man she loves and wants to marry might not be ready—especially at a time when well-meaning friends and family say the engagement period must be a supercharged, happy time in the relationship.

Several times, I had to let go of my cherished dreams for us to be a family, asking God to help my fiancé make the best decision for himself and his purpose in life. That included holding back tears and telling him as calmly as I could that he could still walk away without reproach or guilt.

I also had to fight back against insecurities that could hamper my ability to be the best partner and friend my beloved needed. There were plenty of failed efforts on my part, but I learned to rely on Jesus Christ. I worked to remain faithful to whatever decision he gave to both of us in our hearts.

The engagement period also was tough because it was sink-or-swim for us—I wasn't allowing us to go back to the dating relationship we had. We had been together for more than two years, with the assumption of a stronger commitment. I knew I had to hold to my inner convictions for marriage, which I believed were guided by the Holy Spirit.

Mercifully, we resolved to create a strong marriage, and I believe those agonizing moments during our engagement made us stronger and happier. We were forced to communicate more because our futures were on the line. That's why I urge brides not to worry if there are uncomfortable times during the engagement. It doesn't automatically mean that either person is bailing or the relationship has failed.

Just as he does in purgatory, I believe God has to burn through some of our natural self-centered tendencies to teach us how to love another person with sacrificial love. That's the kind of love in which the couple helps each other get to heaven.

God shows us in trying times how he can create miracles out of our frustration and anxiety. When we trust in him, we know in our guts (in our souls) if we've found the right match. I did, and I'm still awe-inspired today how my Protestant husband draws me closer to the Catholic faith through his own spiritual exploration.

We're just celebrating our first anniversary, and I'm excited about our journey together as we build our family and, above all, help each other get closer to Christ.

If, through the process of courtship, you affirm your shared values and your commitment to be faithful friends for life, the two of you are ready to come before the altar of God to give yourselves freely and totally to each other. With your vows, you bestow upon each other the exalted office of husband and wife. Secure in the irrevocable covenant of marriage, you then consummate your pledge of total self-giving love through the exchange of marital intercourse. It is a blessed union, and it is well worth waiting for.

Through this union, as we have seen, you are prepared to bestow upon each other—God willing and at the right time—the still more exalted office of father and mother, of co-creators with God of a new human being, called to eternal life. This is the greatest gift you can give to each other, except for the gift of salvation itself. And, as husband and wife, you will also help bring the salvation of Christ to each other and to your children.

Creating Your Love Story

1. Look over the "stairway chart" at the beginning of this chapter. Do you think there is a right order in relationships? Have the two of you found that right order? If not, what do you need to do to straighten out your path?

2. As an engaged couple, what internal and external challenges do you think you might face by deciding to save—or resave—sexual intimacy for marriage? Discuss what could provide the best supports for strengthening this commitment. Praying together more often? The sacraments? A sense of humor? Being more selective about what types of TV shows and movies you watch? Socializing more with supportive Christian friends? Finding ways you are comfortable with to explain your choice to people who don't understand it?

3. Make a list of things you would like to do during the sometimes trying but also wonderful, romantic, unique time of your courtship.

CHAPTER EIGHT

Becoming One Flesh: The Twofold Meaning of Sex

Patent Application #337,773
Sexual Intercourse

MANY PEOPLE IN OUR SOCIETY ACT AS IF SEX were something invented by humans. Can you imagine, for example, the head of research at one of the big consumer-products companies making an urgent call to the corporation president: "Boss, we're onto something big! You're never going to believe it. We're calling it 'sex'—and it's going to sell a tsunami of mouthwash, deodorant, cosmetics, and prophylactics."

The fact is: sex sells. An ever-multiplying array of products from lipsticks to Lamborghinis are sold with the implied promise that they will make you more desirable. Many fertility clinics make money—and erode human dignity—by turning laboratories into technological wombs in which human beings are manufactured and also destroyed by demigods in white lab coats. Pharmaceutical companies grow rich by making sterile the life-giving act of marital intercourse. In trying to make sex consequence-free, however, they have made the very people they purport to serve inconsequential—and interchangeable. Sex used to be private and personal but now is often public and anonymous. It was high-touch and low-tech, but now it is "sexted" on smartphones and shared with abandon on YouTube.

From the beginning of the human race, baby-making has been a passionate personal encounter, usually in the warmth of the marriage bed. Now, for many people, not only has baby-making been dragged into the laboratory, but it is further separated from married love by the use of surrogates, egg donors, and sperm donors. In order to reinvent sex and make money from it, our society has detached sex from its proper setting and its rich, personal meaning. All of this has promoted selfishness and degraded sex. And it naturally has led to the proliferation of the outrageous cruelties of sex trafficking and slavery.

In reality, no human being has ever successfully filed a patent on sex. It is God who created sex and marriage. And if God created them, he has a plan for them, a plan he seeks to share with us if we are willing to listen. Since God is the source of beauty, that plan is beautiful. God's plan will also challenge us to grow, to become better and more loving people, because it is not about profit or power—it is about covenant love.

Selfishness overcomes love; love overcomes selfishness
To understand the beauty of God's design—and the damage done when humans turn away from his plan—we must go back to the beginning. We must return to the Creation stories, which are meant to teach us what it means to be human and to be made in the image of God. When God made Eve and presented her to Adam, Adam cried out in joy, "This one at last is bone of my bones and flesh of my flesh!" (Genesis 2:23). God's foundational work was nearing completion because Adam finally had an equal, one like himself to whom he could give his heart. Presumably, Eve was also delighted to receive the love of her husband and to give herself fully to him in love. In all innocence, they no doubt soon discovered how their bodies were designed for a physical union symbolizing and ratifying their total, self-giving love. And they understood their role in God's ongoing work of creation: they were to be fruitful and multiply, bringing new humans into existence in cooperation with God and raising these children to share in fellowship with God.

Everything was simple and beautiful, governed by pure love. But then Adam and Eve were seduced by the prospect of becoming little gods on their own, able to determine good and evil apart from God. According to St. John Paul II and some of the Church Fathers, in separating themselves from God, our first parents found themselves also alienated from each other, and even within themselves. Sexual intimacy became infected with selfishness. They experienced shame and an erosion of trust, revealed in a sudden need for clothing. They were now inclined to manipulate each other for selfish reasons, to get what they wanted.

This selfish separation from God and each other continues, of course, in our own times. And when we ban God from the bedroom, the beauty of God's design in our lives begins to unravel. The intimate union proper to marriage, so deeply personal and creative that it can give rise to new persons, is re-imagined in ways that tend to be impersonal and destructive. We can see this in many aspects of sexuality in modern life, including the pandemic of pornography. Instead of exercising the discipline to commit himself completely to one unique, irreplaceable woman, a man may prefer to view images of thousands of young, exceptionally beautiful women who make no demands upon him, who never get pregnant or have sour moods. They exist (or so it seems) merely for his pleasure, never placing any limits on what he can do or ask for, and appear at his command, disappearing without complaint when he is done with them.

Sex as self-gift that serves love and life is buried under a habit of sex that isolates and idolizes the self. At first, the stimulation of pornography and the associated release of masturbation may seem like an ideal solution for a young man who desires sex but is wary of commitment. Like other addictive behaviors, however, it doesn't satisfy for long, and its practitioners need bigger jolts—perhaps from indulging in more deviant behavior or including the use of real women with warm bodies—to obtain even temporary relief.

Children are the natural fruit of sex. And when God's design is ignored, it is always the children who suffer the most. Shockingly, the average age for first exposure to pornography in the United States is between eleven and fourteen years old, but statistics reported by the USCCB show that it can happen even earlier: 90 percent of eight-to-sixteen-year-olds have viewed pornography, most of them while doing homework.[1] A child's still-developing brain is particularly sensitive to the powerful reactions stimulated by these images.

The irresponsible behavior of adults costs children dearly in other ways as well. As the chart indicates, from 2008 through 2013, approximately 41 percent of children in the United States were born out of wedlock. And the figure is even higher in other countries, such as the United Kingdom: "The proportion of children born to unmarried [UK] mothers hit a record 47.5 per cent last year [2012], according to the Office for National Statistics. The figure has risen from 25 per cent in 1988 and from just 11 per cent in 1979."[2] These innocent ones are denied the security of a home created by the lifelong commitment of real marriage between their mom and dad. Children can be amazingly resilient, but without the committed union of their mother and father, they suffer on average much higher rates of poverty, disease, dysfunction, and abuse.[3]

Percent of US births to unmarried women

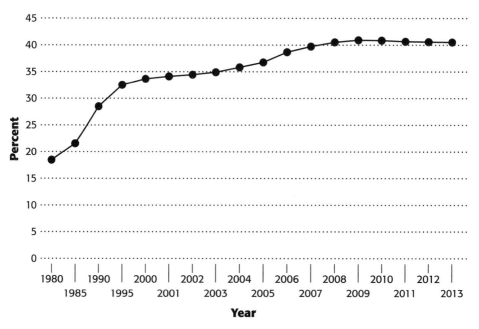

Adapted from *National Vital Statistic Reports*, vol. 64, no.1, January 15, 2015, table B.

The challenge for both engaged and married couples is to rise above society's dysfunctional view of sex and to recapture in a new setting something of the friendship and love that Adam and Eve enjoyed in the Garden of Eden. In search of that innocence and love, let's explore three topics concerning God's plan for sex and marriage:

> Life from union, and union perfected in life
> Sex and the marital covenant
> Children as the fruit of sex

Life from union

The life-giving wonder of God's plan for human sexuality is evident, first of all, in our physiological reproductive characteristics. As a baby girl develops in the womb, she has as many as a million incipient ova, or eggs, in her two ovaries. By the time she is born, the number has dropped to about 250,000. That's still a lot of potential children, even for those who would like a large family. However, only a few hundred eggs will develop to maturity throughout all of a normal, healthy woman's fertile years.

A boy, on the other hand, does not produce any sperm until he reaches puberty, but then his testicles begin producing billions of them every month. At the culmination of intercourse, the seminal fluid that contains these seekers of life is ejaculated from the husband's body into his wife's vagina, and the sperm swim energetically in search of the union that brings life. Typically, the husband deposits near the cervix, the opening to his wife's uterus, an astonishing two hundred million to five hundred million of these tiny competitors in pursuit of life. Some of them carry the X ("girl") gene and others the Y ("boy") gene.

If it is the right time in the woman's cycle, glands in the cervix will produce a type of mucus that welcomes the sperm, nourishing them and opening up swimming channels. Thus fortified and directed, the multitudes of sperm engage in a madhouse competition to swim through the uterus and arrive in the correct fallopian tube at just the opportune moment to meet the one and only ovum released by the wife that month. Out of the hundreds of millions of contestants in this ultimate reality show, there is room for only one triumphant sperm, who may (or may not) win her hand.

If a sperm succeeds in penetrating the ovum's outer membrane, the sperm and egg combine genetic material and instantaneously become a new, unique human being, given an immortal soul by God. This child embodies in one flesh the love of its mother and father. Many characteristics of this tiny girl or boy, such as hair and eye color, potential height, and personality traits, are already determined at the instant of conception. Within five to nine days, this new member of the human race will attach to the lining of the mom's uterus, which is also called the womb. Here beneath its mother's heart, it will find the protection, nutrition, and love it needs for its development. Within twenty-two days of conception, this little girl or boy has its own functioning heart, pumping its own blood through its tiny—and unmistakably human—body.

But what if it is not the right time for conception? What if the ovum of the month is not promenading down the fallopian tube when the husband launches a vast armada of sperm near his wife's cervix? The heroic little tadpoles will find no luxurious carpet rolled out for them, no welcoming, stretchy mucus to provide nutrition and swimming channels. The poor sperm will also find the cervix blocked by a thick mucus plug. The sperm will still seek life with all their being, but even the most valiant among them will not be able to find the ovum of his dreams. Within about twenty-four hours, they will all be spent. No new life will be conceived.

The contrast between one egg and hundreds of millions of sperm corresponds in a way to the two contrasting purposes of sex and marriage according to Christian tradition: the exclusive unity of the spouses and the multiplicity involved in the creation of new life. New life comes forth from the unity of the spouses, and their unity is perfected in and serves that new life.

We could say, in the strange mathematics of love, that $1 + 1 = 1$ (unity of the spouses) so that $1 + 1 = 3^+$ (the conception of new life). These two purposes of sex and marriage are so intertwined that they cannot be pulled apart without damage to both.

Sexual union as a renewal of the marriage covenant

John Kippley, the co-founder of the Couple to Couple League, developed a biblically based formula to describe the inherent meaning of sexual intercourse that includes both unity and new life. In his book *Sex and the Marriage Covenant: A Basis for Morality,* he wrote, "Sexual intercourse is intended by God to be at least implicitly a renewal of the marriage covenant."[4] As we have already seen, a covenant is a radical, binding relationship, typically sealed by a ritual action or a sacrifice. The Old Covenant between God and his people, for example, was sealed with the sprinkling of bull's blood, a symbol both of death and of shared life. The New Covenant was sealed by the blood of Jesus on the Cross. The covenant of marriage is formed by a couple's wedding vows and is sealed in the total self-giving of the marital embrace, especially in the exchange of seminal fluid from husband to wife. That's what intercourse means—it is a ratification and renewal of the marriage covenant in which husband and wife enter into a life-changing relationship, promising before God and the community to give themselves, and to receive the other, freely, totally, faithfully, and fruitfully.

The notion of sex as a renewal of the marriage covenant helps to explain the positive meaning of the "rules" around sex. Sexual intimacy should be exclusive to marriage, for example, because before or outside of marriage, there is no covenant to renew. Adultery is even worse because it betrays the marriage covenant by means of the very act meant to continually renew it. Masturbation, mutual or solo; condoms, hormonal pills, patches, or shots; diaphragms, spermicides, and sterilization all attempt to prevent or counteract the exchange that ratifies the marriage covenant. But a couple cannot actively exclude God's gift of fertility without also excluding God's active presence in deepening their bond.

Understanding marriage as a covenant can help you live up to the ideals of marriage. On your wedding day, you stand before God's altar and promise to give yourselves totally to each other for the rest of your lives. In marital intercourse, that very same commitment takes a bodily form. In the language of the body, as designed by God, the husband says in effect to his wife: "With this gift of my whole body—and especially that which I will never share with anyone else, my semen—I give you all of myself: my life, my ability to *give* life, my future, my whole being. And in your reception of me, I accept the gift of your life and future, your body and soul, for richer or poorer, for better or worse." The wife says with her body, "In receiving you and your seed, I willingly accept what I will never receive from anyone else. I welcome your whole self, your life and future, your body and soul, and I give my whole self to you in return. Your life is now my life, and my life is now your life. Any children I bear will be our children."

To be consistent, of course, this giving of self and receiving of one's spouse must not be reserved exclusively for the bedroom but should be expressed in all aspects of marriage. That's why many wives find it downright romantic when their husbands willingly help with the laundry and the cooking. It is a well-established fact, furthermore, that no husband was ever shot while doing the dishes. Wives also need to respect—and celebrate!—the work, the skill, and the sacrifices of their husbands. This sharing of life ain't easy. It requires constant effort—and constant forgiveness, assisted by grace and the sacraments of Confession and Eucharist. Whether we bargained for it or not, marriage and family life is a school of holiness, complete with pop quizzes every day.

Sexual union for the creation of new life

As an eternal sign of the union of its mom and dad, a child is meant to have the security of coming forth into the world in the context of a community of love created by the foundational bond of marriage. The point here is that this mystery of love flows in both directions: a child is the ultimate sign and fruit of the union of the spouses, and the union of the spouses is necessary to create the loving environment in which kids thrive. A child may have the wife's dark hair, exuberant personality, and flat feet. That same child may have the husband's love of sports, musical ability, and lanky build. But these attributes inherited from each of the parents are united in one person. Unity prepares for children; children celebrate and deepen union. Two become one so that two can become three in unanimity.

Thus, husband and wife become one flesh on three levels: (1) in their marriage, especially as expressed in sexual intercourse, (2) in their children, and (3) in their shared faith by which they make their family into a school of love in union with Christ.

Husband patiently leads wife, wife patiently leads husband

In marital intercourse, the giving of pleasure and the receiving of pleasure become indistinguishable. This forms a metaphor, if you will, for mutual love, in which the giving is also a receiving, and the receiving is also a giving. Sexual intimacy in marriage is a deeply human act that involves body and soul, sacrifice and pleasure, exclusive commitment and, as we shall see more clearly in the next chapter, openness to life.

It is often the case that a man must learn how to lead his wife patiently, gently, and kindly into physical intimacy, discovering how different she is from him and learning what works and what doesn't work for her. A woman, on the other hand, often leads her husband patiently, gently, and kindly into emotional intimacy. She learns to discuss things that interest him, even if she is not smitten with the wonders of a particular model of internal combustion engine or the brilliant defensive strategy of the Real Madrid soccer team. This generous willingness to attend to his interests builds trust and makes it easier for the husband to share vulnerable feelings, hopes, and fears, which is so vital to the friendship of marriage. Emotional intimacy and sexual intimacy go together like . . . well, like wife and husband, who are meant to become one in a tender, loving union.

If one of the leading consumer product companies had invented sex, as we imagined at the beginning of this chapter, it would not be nearly as wonderful—or as occasionally comical—as it actually is. Just as eating and drinking are necessary for the life of individuals, so sexual intercourse is necessary for the life of the species. These three functions are very much a part of the life of the body, but we may feel at times that they lack a certain delicacy. Sometimes they stand in humorous contrast to our dignity as spiritual persons, yet God has elevated eating and drinking to the spiritual heights in Holy Communion, where we become one with him in the most glorious way possible on earth. And he has exalted sexual intercourse within the sacrament of marriage to become a remarkable expression of love—a human love that, like divine love, opens to life.

Creating Your Love Story

1. Discuss the ways in which our culture may have shaped your understanding of sexuality. How have TV, films, music, print media, fashion, advertising, or any exposure to pornography in the past influenced you? How is the deeply personal understanding of sex and marriage taught by the Church shifting your perceptions as you read this book?

2. Discuss what sex—speaking in the language of the body—is intended to say. If you are already married, does your lovemaking speak of this total self-gift? What can you do to make your sexual intimacy deeper and more authentic?

3. Describe the kind of parent each of you wants to be, and consider what skills and character traits you need to develop to be that kind of parent.

CHAPTER NINE

The Seasons
of Married Life
Natural Family Planning

AS I MENTIONED IN THE PREFACE, when my wife and I were married, we knew that the Church had some sort of teaching against contraception, but it seemed to be a lingering relic of ancient times and certainly not a practical requirement for modern Catholics. Because we were dependent on my wife's income while I was working for low pay at a startup, having children seemed impractical, if not outright irresponsible. All the Catholic couples we knew used contraception. We had no qualms about it—it seemed as normal as brushing our teeth. It certainly never occurred to either of us to mention it when we went to Confession.

A year later, a friend lent us a copy of *Humanae Vitae*. It was the most devastating thing we had ever read. As Catholics, we accepted that Jesus speaks to us through the Apostles and through their successors, the bishops, when they teach in union with the Pope as the successor of St. Peter. This is what Jesus meant when he told his Apostles, "Whoever listens to you listens to me" (Luke 10:16). We therefore could not, as *Humanae Vitae* states, "determine in a wholly autonomous way the honest path to follow" once we understood that "couples must conform their activity to the creative intention of God, expressed in the very nature of marriage and of its acts, and manifested by the constant teaching of the church."[1]

After deep prayer, no little struggle, and, it must be admitted, some whining, we agreed to give up contraceptives and to learn Natural Family Planning out of obedience to Jesus. But it felt like the heaviest cross ever thrust upon us. Contraceptives seemed so easy, and Natural Family Planning was hard at first. My wife was anxious about getting pregnant before we were ready, and I sometimes found it extremely difficult to abstain during the fertile time in each cycle. The method of Natural Family Planning we first learned depends on a single sign of fertility that works well for the vast majority of couples. But it didn't work so well for us. Our plans and our sense of control were shattered by a surprise pregnancy—our first son (we like to say that he is still surprising us today!). The shock of the pregnancy precipitated a crisis.

As conflicted as we were, however, we both realized that the Holy Spirit had burned the bridge behind us and we could not turn back. To our amazement, in the nine months after we placed the contraceptives in the trash and relied on Natural Family Planning, our relationship improved. We had thought we had a great marriage, but it was clear in retrospect that contraception had involved exploitation, especially in my use of my wife to satisfy desire. Cooperating with the cycle of fertility that God had designed, on the other hand, was an act of respect and love that we wanted to continue.

Fortified by prayer, we welcomed our first beautiful boy into the world, and God came to our assistance. We discovered St. John Paul II's Theology of the Body, which gave us a profound vision of the self-giving love of marriage. We also found another method of Natural Family Planning that was easier for us. It was like driving north on the Golden Gate Bridge and emerging out of the San Francisco fog and into the sunshine.

We should not have been surprised that Christian marriage leads to the cross. Anything that shares in the sacrifice of Christ will require repentance, faith, self-mastery, and self-giving. Nor should we have been surprised that Jesus would help us along the way and that this cross would lead to new and more abundant life. That is the resurrection.

As my wife and I discovered, Natural Family Planning helps bring couples into harmony with the law of love and life that God has written into our very being and into the nature of Christian marriage. What is really surprising is that this truth has been kept so devastatingly well hidden. Since Patricia and I began to teach Natural Family Planning through the Couple to Couple League in 1985, we have witnessed many couples discovering and maturing in a more profound married love through NFP.

A challenging but liberating truth

You may have seen one of the iconic photographs of two bitter enemies, Nelson Mandela and F. W. de Klerk, when the latter was president of South Africa; the two are shaking hands to confirm the historic agreement to end white minority rule. But imagine if either Mandela or de Klerk had slipped on a plastic glove before shaking hands. It's pretty obvious that the plastic glove would have completely subverted the positive symbolism.

We can understand the implied meaning of a handshake in any encounter—the act of shaking hands is rich in meaning because our hands are an essential part of our humanness, and most human work involves our hands. A handshake, therefore, affirms our shared humanity and a commitment to work together. But many people may no longer even want to understand the inherent significance of the most intimate and meaningful encounter of all, marital intercourse. People avert their eyes to avoid seeing how strange it really is to engage in the ultimate act of union while utilizing technological gadgets, surgical interventions, or synthetic hormones to counteract that union. Marital intercourse is not merely a symbol like a handshake; it actually accomplishes something momentous. The act of sowing the husband's seed in the wife's reproductive system reveals that love gives life, and life is perfected in love. They entrust their body, soul, and future to each other, renewing the total giving pledged in their wedding vows. We could say that marital intercourse is designed by God as his invitation to us to say "Yes!" to three things:

YES! . . . to the complete unity of husband and wife as promised at your wedding

YES! . . . to the possibility of children

YES! . . . to the presence in your marriage of the self-giving love of Jesus for his Bride, the Church

But the fact is that we don't always *want* to know such ennobling truths. It often seems easier to go with the flow of our drives and desires. And there is plenty of support in the culture—especially in the media—for the idea that we can have whatever we want and do whatever we like. As one example among millions, the bright red cover of the August 2014 issue of *Psychology Today* magazine had this message emblazoned on it:

LOVE & LUST
Yes, You Can Have It All!
* BUT BEWARE
THE KIDDIE TRAP

Chastity places sexual desire at the service of love and thereby shows a great respect for other people and fosters ever-deeper intimacy. Lust, on the other hand, unleashes sexual desire to serve selfishness and uses other people in a demeaning way that is not compatible with love. And babies become the enemies! In the case of this article, the headline may have been worse than the content, but both exhibit the exploitative attitude that St. John Paul II described as a "contraceptive mentality" that leads to a culture of death. To treat your spouse with the love and respect due to a person made in the image of God is a great challenge, but it draws both you and your spouse to each other and to God. Natural Family Planning is an important aid in this grace-filled process.

What is Natural Family Planning?
NFP is a type of knowledge, a knowledge of your bodies and your shared fertility as a married couple, as well as a knowledge of God's plan for married life. At first, it can seem as though God's program, revealed through the Church, was an external, intrusive restriction that could interfere with the expression of your love. It is, in fact, exactly the opposite: it liberates couples to love more deeply. God has written a law of love into our bodies and into our souls. And even though it is not easy to live according to this exalted law, when we seek his will, God shows us the surpassing beauty of human love touched by divine love.

The first requirement for Natural Family Planning is a willingness to determine, through reason and prayer, when it is right to seek (or simply not avoid) conception, and when it is right to postpone it. Christ teaches through the Church that couples should not take a rain check on this miracle for trivial or selfish reasons. The *Catechism of the Catholic Church* requires "just reasons" to postpone pregnancy (*CCC* 2368). This means that a couple should consider what is due to God, to each other, to their already existing children, and to other people that God brings into their lives, especially those in need. In this process, it is legitimate for a couple to consider their physical and mental health, current economic conditions, and other important responsibilities, prayerfully and prudently weighing the challenges they face.

Love always supports life, but sometimes, for just reasons, a couple's lovemaking may not be actively directed to conception. Or conception may be highly unlikely due to the phase of the fertility cycle or other natural factors, such as advancing age. There may also be times of potential fertility when it is right for a couple to practice abstinence to postpone pregnancy for a while, or even for an indefinite period. As they ponder the various factors involved, it is important to keep in mind the greatness of the opportunity to share with God in the creation of a new human being and to remember that this opportunity fades with time. It's also good to remember that a new brother or sister is often by far the best gift a couple can give their existing children.

It is in accordance with God's plan that couples should use their reason, together with prayer, to make wise, prudential judgments about family size and spacing, as long as they have an appropriate appreciation of the gift of fertility and respect the integrity of the marital act. To act directly against (contra) conception in order to eliminate the potential of love giving rise to life interferes with the way God has made us, and it sterilizes sexual intimacy, reducing it to a self-serving use of the other person.

It is true that couples can selfishly use the knowledge of the fertility cycle to avoid conception for trivial reasons. It is inaccurate, however, to equate selfish avoidance with the grave wrong of contraception. Consider a parallel situation, in which two Christians both fall short of the gospel mandate to help the poor. The first Christian is stingy and does not devote the time or treasure that he reasonably could. The other actively cheats workers out of wages, knowing that his employees are undocumented and have no recourse. Obviously, a lack of generosity must be addressed and corrected in both cases. Equally obvious, the active exploitation of the poor is a crime of far greater magnitude. The *Catechism of the Catholic Church* quotes St. John Paul II in this regard: "The difference . . . between contraception and recourse to the rhythm of the cycle . . . involves in the final analysis two irreconcilable concepts of the human person and of human sexuality" (*CCC* 2370).

Welcoming the seasons of life

We are all thoroughly familiar with the cycle of the seasons, which is closely linked to the fertility of nature and to the conception and growth of all forms of life. We can always tell where we are in the progression of the seasons by the signs that nature gives us. In a similar way, a woman's body cycles through a regular pattern of "seasons" of fertility and infertility each month. While contraception works to repress and override the springtime of fertility, Natural Family Planning responds to and works with the natural order of the seasons.

The best way to learn Natural Family Planning (NFP) is through a class with a well-trained teaching couple who know the technique through personal experience and also are aware of the spiritual and marital dynamics involved. The Couple to Couple League has taught NFP to approximately half a million people across all fifty states and in a number of foreign countries. The information is presented in a series of three classes, spaced about a month apart, which allows couples to practice observing and charting through a few cycles. Classes are available in person or online. (See the resource list for information on CCL and other reputable NFP organizations.)

With a little guidance, you can easily learn how to observe and interpret the natural signs produced by the hormones that govern a woman's cycle and

The Seasons of Fertility and Married Life

Seasons	Signs of the Season	Signs of Wife's Cycle	Female Hormones	Fertile or Infertile: State of Body
Autumn	Leaves redden and fall; an end and a beginning	Monthly period	Progesterone drops	Infertile while the wife's body cleans out remnants of last cycle, readying for next
Winter	Cold, dry; nature at rest	No mucus and low temperature	Both estrogen and progesterone low	Infertile interlude before the action starts
Spring	Sap begins to flow; nature is fertile	Mucus appears and temperatures are still low	Estrogen builds up, leading to egg release	Fertile time to make babies! (or to abstain if you have a just reason to postpone pregnancy)
Summer	Dry, and temps up as nature nurtures what has been conceived	Mucus dries up and temperatures are up	Progesterone elevated; estrogen falls	Infertile time when the wife's body shifts out of conception mode into nurture mode, if a baby has been conceived

identify what "season" you are in at any given time. This involves observing and charting the changes in the wife's basal body temperature (temperature at rest after a night's sleep) and/or observing her mucus pattern and perhaps other signs. You can use this information to time sexual relations for maximum fertility if you are ready to participate with God in the conception of a child. If you are seeking to avoid pregnancy for the time being, you can observe the same symptoms and restrict your relations to infertile times, when conception is highly unlikely.

Observing the temperature takes just a few seconds every morning. The thermometer retains the reading so that it can be noted on a chart later. The mucus observation takes a few seconds every time the woman uses the bathroom. The temperature and/or mucus signs are noted on either a paper chart or an e-chart on a computer or smartphone. The patterns on the chart, interpreted by certain rules, indicate whether the woman is in the pre-ovulation infertile time, the fertile time around ovulation, or the post-ovulation infertile time.

The greatest challenge
For many couples, the greatest challenge in NFP is the need to avoid marital intercourse during the fertile times when a couple discerns well-grounded reasons to postpone pregnancy. For most couples, most of the time, the period of abstinence is about nine to twelve days per cycle of roughly twenty-eight days. Longer periods of abstinence may be required, however, for some couples or in special situations, such as when a woman's fertility is returning after childbirth or fading away as menopause approaches. Abstinence can be a real trial, especially in an instant-gratification culture. And it is true that women often experience maximum physical desire during the fertile time, when it is necessary to abstain if avoiding pregnancy. This also can be a challenge—but at least it is a more natural challenge than the reduction of desire, weight gain, depression, and other side effects experienced by many women who use hormonal contraceptives.

Some couples may be tempted to use a condom or other contraceptives during these times or to engage in mutual masturbation. First of all, the number of surprise pregnancies due to failed condom use during the fertile time is high. With or without a condom, any genital contact at those times can result in pregnancy even if the couple avoids the full act of intercourse. But even if that were not the case, contraceptives interfere with the self-giving of wife and husband; and masturbation, which is any stimulation intended to produce orgasm without depositing the husband's seed in the wife's vagina, is a disconnection that contradicts the unity of marriage.

Being faithful out of respect for God and respect for one's spouse always has spiritual benefits as well. Some couples have found that their relationship is kept fresh by a regular cycle of courtship (times of abstinence) and honeymoon (times of consummation). Others discover that the need for periodic abstinence has encouraged them to develop their friendship in a variety of new ways, enriching their marriage. They may, for example, go out on dates during times of abstinence and learn to talk more deeply, like when they were first falling in love. It also helps couples to realize that their sexual desire is in fact a desire for union that reaches beyond the physical and even beyond themselves. Ultimately, all real love comes from God and leads us back to God.

When is it okay to use NFP to postpone pregnancy?

Let's end this chapter with one more look at the sometimes perplexing question of when it is okay to use NFP to postpone pregnancy. Consider another parallel: when is it okay to spend money on anything other than basic necessities, supporting the Church, and helping the poor? The Church offers guidelines rather than strict rules, encouraging us to exercise prudential judgment and reflect God's great generosity. The same is true concerning family size and spacing the conception of children. But the guidelines are clear: we are called to respect the integrity of the marriage act, to be generous in the service of life, and to remember the greatness of sharing in God's highest act of creation. In this context, each couple must pray and consider their own circumstances and decide how God is leading them.

Imagine a couple who married in medical school and now have more than a hundred thousand dollars in student debt between them. They are headed for several years of internship and residency before they can enter the workforce. Family and friends have strongly suggested that the wife get a shot or a patch or pop some long-acting pills and take kids out of the equation for a while. The couple themselves, however, feel uncomfortable with powerful, artificial hormones that override the woman's natural cycle. They also know how these contraceptive hormones, excreted in the urine of women using hormonal birth control, pass into rivers and lakes, where they can cause sexual deformities in freshwater fish.[2] Both of them resonate with Church teaching that life cannot be actively divorced from love without repercussions.

So what can they do? This couple's reasons for postponing conception are certainly not trivial. They would be wise to talk with each other about their hopes and fears, their obligations and aspirations. They should take their situation to God in prayer and in trust, and perhaps also consult a priest or other spiritual advisor whom they can rely on to offer guidance in accordance with the authentic teachings of Christ through the Church.

In sum, a couple who are evaluating their circumstances with reason, faith, generosity, and prayer need not seek a baby every time they engage in the self-giving proper to marriage. But they must not alter themselves with a surgeon's knife, with artificial hormones, with the introduction of physical barriers, or by intentionally spilling the man's seed outside the wife's reproductive system, in order to frustrate the life-giving power that God has woven into the physical self-gift of married couples. God has united wife and husband as one flesh in marriage in order for them to share in a love that is so full of life that it can naturally result in new life. This is a miraculous gift. St. Paul tells us in the letter to the Ephesians that this love between husband and wife refers to the mystery of Jesus and his Bride, the Church (Ephesians 5:21–32). Jesus makes a complete gift of himself—body, soul, and divinity—especially on the Cross; the Church, in turn, makes a total gift of herself to Jesus, placing herself completely at his disposal. This mutual giving is never a closed circle; it is always open to life, leading Christians into a deeper union with Christ and bringing life to those in need, especially those who have been enemies of Christ.

We are called to faithfully and consistently aim for the highest expression of God's plan for marriage and family life, and to understand how our choices bear witness to the gospel. But in the context of our culture, even the selfish use of Natural Family Planning is a huge step in the right direction for most couples. Engaging in a sincere, dedicated struggle toward self-mastery, respect for each other, and respect for God's design—this is the path of love, patience, and kindness. Facing these challenges together as a couple will open your hearts to the greatness of participating with God in the creation of new human beings.

Not long ago, Ronald and Kelly Brock could never have imagined that they would become a CCL teaching couple. Now they enjoy sharing their love story with the couples who attend their Natural Family Planning classes.

> *Ron:* Growing up, I was taught about safe sex and waiting until marriage to be intimate, but nobody told me what happens *after* you get married. For the first few years we were together, Kelly and I tried a mix of hormonal and barrier methods, but we figured that getting pregnant was unlikely, because Kelly had only one ovary and had polycystic ovarian syndrome. But we played it safe just in case. I always kind of assumed it was Kelly's responsibility to prevent a pregnancy by taking the Pill.

> *Kelly:* I was introduced to the Pill when I was twelve as a means to combat acne. For the ten-plus years I was on and off the Pill, my skin looked great and my cycles were regular, but I struggled with migraine headaches,

nausea and vomiting, and weight gain. After the birth of our second child, I told my ob-gyn, who is an NFP supporter, that I didn't want to put any drugs in my body, and that I wasn't comfortable with most barrier methods. With oral contraception and barrier methods (other than condoms) off the table, I wanted to know what my options were.

Not knowing my religious views, and not wanting to turn me off by suggesting Natural Family Planning (which I, as a Protestant, thought of as just "Catholic birth control" at the time), he suggested I order a book about fertility awareness from a secular point of view and start learning the sympto-thermal method. I read that book from cover to cover.

I was actually excited about this natural method and surprised that with all the "sex talks" I sat through in high school, I had never heard the truth about my fertility. Going natural was important to me because over the previous three years, I had lost 115 pounds, adopted a lifestyle free of refined sugars and flour and processed foods, and was training for my first half-marathon. The last thing I wanted was to go back on the Pill. When I told a friend of mine about the sympto-thermal method, she said, "Oh, that's the same thing as NFP!" She had taken a class with her husband when they were engaged, and she gave me her old NFP book and some blank charts.

Ron: We soon realized that the only difference between the methods in these two books was that the NFP book suggested that couples abstain on fertile days. We laughed it off at the time, but Kelly kept turning back to the NFP book to read the quotes about God's design for our bodies and the union with our spouse as "life-giving and love-giving." Many of the quotes came from Pope John Paul II and his book on the Theology of the Body, which we were skeptical about reading. I had plenty of preconceived notions about Catholicism, but I was happy to see what Kelly was interested in.

Kelly suggested we take the NFP class just to make sure we were "doing it right." She contacted the Couple to Couple League to find a teacher in our area, but the class would not be starting for several months. Because Kelly was postpartum with our second child and nursing while trying to learn NFP, the "rules" were different, so the teaching couple suggested that we meet sooner. Kelly sent them an e-mail to say she was interested in talking about the theology behind NFP. They suggested *Theology of the Body (TOBB) for Beginners*, by Christopher West. Hesitantly, we ordered it that night, and when it came, we read it together.

Kelly: Around this time, I went back to my gynecologist. He knew that Ron and I were trying to learn the sympto-thermal method. After he had looked at my charts, he casually reminded us to abstain on fertile days, as if it were common knowledge. "Abstain on fertile days?" I thought. "That's terrible! We abstained (mostly) for the five years prior to getting married, and now we'd have to abstain for part of every cycle?"

My doctor didn't say this in an accusatory or shaming way, but it was purposeful. The Holy Spirit was convincing me—and in a doctor's office, of all places!

Ron: A few weeks later, we met with the CCL teaching couple. While we were going over our charts, the conversation revolved mostly around how NFP had saved their marriage. Even though Kelly and I were content in our marriage, we knew for certain that in the months following our second child's birth, we had grown even closer in many ways. We felt that most of it could be attributed to this new method, but we didn't understand why. We talked about what we had been reading in *TOBB* and about other Catholic teachings that seemed so foreign to two Protestants.

Kelly: I didn't know if I agreed completely with the Church's teachings on contraception, but I thought to myself, "What harm could come by exercising some self-control throughout the month?" If it was natural and helped Ron and me to respect our bodies and fertility, then it couldn't hurt to abstain periodically.

Ron: I had no idea how to feel when Kelly asked if we could try abstaining for one month to see how it worked, but before the first month was over, we had already seen a drastic change in our marriage. It was like nothing we had ever experienced. I noticed the change in Kelly's mood, and since we were no longer using any artificial methods of birth control, our love life, and the closeness of our relationship and communication, totally changed for the better. We'd been married eight years at that point, and it seemed like we finally started to figure things out.

Kelly: When I was in junior high, I made a promise to God to remain sexually pure until I got married. Ron knew how I felt and understood why God wanted that for us. However, over the five years we were together before getting married, I was unable to keep my promise. I enjoyed what we were doing and loved Ron, but I began to feel disappointed in myself, to feel trapped and used. At times I told myself it was okay, because Ron said he wanted to marry me. But I knew in my heart that saying yes to Ron meant saying no to God's will for my life.

After we got married, I thought the guilt I had been feeling regarding our premarital relations would go away, but it didn't. As I read *TOBB* and the NFP book, I thought the vision of marital intimacy presented in them sounded like a fairytale. I started to get angry and thought, "This has to have been written by someone who's never had sex! Only couples who remained sexually pure before they got married could have this kind of intimacy in their marriage. I'll never have this with Ron." But something amazing happened in that first month of trying NFP. It was as if Ron and I had been given a second chance.

Ron: I had no idea how this was playing out in Kelly's heart, but I knew that my wife had changed for the better. When Kelly was on birth control, she had no sexual desire and did not feel feminine, nor did she have maternal feelings or urges. For the first four years of our marriage, she thought there was something wrong with her. In order to spice things up, we tried pornography to try to rekindle the passions we'd had when we were younger. It didn't work the way we had hoped, and we have since removed it from our home. After Kelly stopped taking oral contraception, though, everything changed.

Kelly: I felt frustrated that I had wasted so much time abusing my body and that Ron and I had unknowingly been degrading our relationship with each other—and, ultimately, with God. After eight years of marriage, we finally understood what God intended for us. More importantly, because of the grace given to me through the sacrament of Reconciliation, the years of guilt and hurt I carried about our premarital relations and use of pornography started to fade.

Ron: Much of the work falls on Kelly in practicing NFP, but that doesn't mean that I don't play a part. For example, when I get up in the morning, I'll wake her up so she can take her temperature at the same time every day. Also, we leave our NFP chart open next to our bed so that I can see where we are in the cycle. It's just another way of being in communication throughout each cycle. NFP also requires me to trust my wife more, since Kelly's the one observing her mucus throughout the day. I have to trust that she understands what she's observing. And there are times when we look at the chart together to determine if we have started phase three or if we need to wait another day!

Kelly: To be honest, though, abstaining can be difficult. When we were phasing out condoms to use NFP exclusively, it was a tense time for us. I already knew that I did not want to use condoms anymore. No fault of Ron's . . . but to be honest, sex was never really that good for me when we used a condom. It felt sterile, uncomfortable, and lacking in any real sensation. It was worth it to wait a few extra days and then get to have really great sex rather than cashing in early and only having okay sex.

Ron: It was difficult for a while, but knowing that my wife was enjoying our intimacy so much more gave me greater satisfaction as well. Kelly and I took a quiz once that told us what each of our love languages is. My main way of receiving and feeling love (this should come as no surprise) is through physical contact; but Kelly's main way is through quality time. So, in order to show Kelly in a nonsexual way that I love her, we will set aside a date night, even if it's just putting the kids to bed early and making dinner for the two of us. This allows me to give my full attention to my wife and to talk about things that are important to her and our family. Quality time can also be as simple as cuddling on the couch with a glass of wine and catching up on our DVR recordings.

Kelly: Though Ron's main love language is physical contact, that doesn't necessarily mean sex. For example, I know he likes it when I put my hand on his arm or leg while we're watching TV or in the car. I also know that he loves having his head and neck massaged. Those are easy things I can do during times of abstinence to show I love him. But sometimes we like to spend those few days of abstinence flirting with each other, like we used to when we first met. Even though we can't do anything sexual, a few days of flirting gives us something great to look forward to.

Sometimes it's difficult to explain to people, but the truth is that when Ron and I chose to do NFP and abstain, we weren't saying no to sex. We were saying yes to better sex—sex that feels mutual, that shows respect toward each other's bodies. That's what has brought us closer together as husband and wife—and it has been ultimately more gratifying than anything we experienced before. We lived for so long asking God to be in our hearts but not allowing Him into our bedroom. With NFP, God is welcome in both places, and it has taught us to have total trust in Him.

Creating Your Love Story

1. How far along are you in the process of developing the virtues and self-mastery that allow you to give yourself generously to your spouse?

2. How do you feel about the opportunity to cooperate with God in the creation and salvation of a new human person? Have you talked about how many children you each desire and whether adoption would be an option for you?

3. What, in your opinion, would be examples of good reasons to postpone pregnancy or to seek pregnancy?

4. When the Brocks started using NFP in their marriage, they experienced what felt to them to be a second chance for intimacy and sexual purity. Do you need a second chance? If so, what would a second chance look like for you?

CHAPTER TEN

The Sacrament of Marriage and the Life of God

MOST MARRIED CHRISTIANS ARE ONLY HAZILY AWARE of the mysteries of which they are a part. But it is liberating to know that hidden under the daily trivialities and trials of marriage is something supremely good and beautiful: a sharing in the sacrifice of Jesus and in the life of the Trinity. Let's zip up our theological G-suits for a quick trip to the heights to get a glimpse of the mystery of sacramental marriage as a sharing in the life of God.

The sacraments: Fountains of life

In ancient Israel, it was thought that people with leprosy were under God's judgment. Lepers not only were afflicted with an incurable disease that deadens nerve endings and often results in the loss of hands, feet, facial features, or other body parts, but also were cut off from family and friends. The Gospels tell us about a leper who came up to Jesus, bowed down before him, and begged for healing (Matthew 8:1–4; Luke 5:12–16). Jesus responded in a way far beyond what any doctor would do, touching the leper and making him clean by, in effect, taking the isolation and leprosy upon himself. This is what Jesus does to heal us from the spiritual leprosy of sin. In a marvelous exchange, he takes upon himself the eternal consequences of our rebellion against God so that he can share with us the joy that flows from his perfect obedience to the Father. Jesus is still touching people like you and me, overcoming our isolation and making us clean. He works this exchange through his sacrifice on the Cross, which he makes present to us above all in the sacraments.

To receive one of the seven sacraments, which were established by Christ, is to receive the healing and sanctifying touch of Jesus himself. The *Catechism of the Catholic Church* says that the sacraments are "perceptible signs (words and actions) accessible to our human nature. By the action of Christ and the power of the Holy Spirit they make present efficaciously the grace that they signify" (*CCC* 1084). They are "powers that come forth" from the Body of Christ, "the master works of God in the new and everlasting covenant" (*CCC* 1116). The life-giving sacraments at work in the Body of Christ allow us to overcome the isolation of sin, develop virtue, and enter into friendship with God and one another.

If a baptized Christian properly marries another baptized Christian, their marriage is recognized by the Catholic Church as a sacrament. As agents of Christ, the bride and groom actually bestow this sacrament on each other, and they become for the rest of their lives a sacrament to one another. To explore the beauty and depth of what this means for your love story, let's consider the nature of the sacraments. The best approach is through the Cross of Christ.

Pictured here is the famous cross of St. Francis, called the San Damiano cross because it originally hung in the little chapel of San Damiano just below the hillside town of Assisi, Italy. It was from this cross that Jesus spoke to St. Francis, commanding him to "rebuild my church." Francis immediately began to reconstruct the little chapel, which was falling apart. It later became clear, however, that Jesus was calling St. Francis to help rebuild not only a small chapel in Italy but also the entire Catholic Church through the world, which was in grave need of reform. (This is why Pope Francis took the name of this great saint; like St. Francis, he wants to rebuild the Church through a return to the love and simplicity of Christ.)

Almost all modern crucifixes show the body of Jesus on the Cross after he has died. This medieval cross, however, shows Jesus alive but not in apparent agony. The image combines the crucified and the resurrected Christ, revealing Jesus, dead and risen, as he continues his presence in our world through us—his people—and his Church. If you look closely at the wounds in our Lord's side, feet, and hands, you can see a little fountain of blood spurting forth from each wound. The Jewish people have always believed that life is in the blood. That is why, under Mosaic Law, the blood of animals could not be consumed. Blood belongs to God, who alone gives life. In the New Covenant, however, the bloody wounds of Jesus have become fountains of life, through which our wounds are healed and we share in the life of God. As a way to explore the vocation of marriage in the context of all seven sacraments, we can associate each of the wounds with a specific sacrament.

The Seven Sacraments		
Sacrament	**Corresponding Wound**	**Application to Death and Resurrection**
Baptism	Spear wound in side	Cleansing of sin and entry into the Church
Eucharist	Spear wound in side	Jesus's self-gift through the Cross
Reconciliation	Right foot	Cleansing of post-baptismal sin
Anointing of the Sick	Left foot	Healing of body (sickness) and soul (sin)
Ordination	Right hand	Service of Christ's Bride, the Church
Marriage	Left hand	Service of spouse, kids, Church, society
Confirmation	Head	Full incorporation into the work of Christ

The Gospel of John tells us that water and blood flow from the spear wound in the right **side** of Jesus. The water and the blood have always been associated with the two greatest sacraments, *Baptism* and the *Eucharist*, which flow from the pierced heart of our Lord. It is by baptism in water that we are first cleansed from sin and enter into the community of the Church. The blood represents the Eucharist, the greatest of all the sacraments, making present to us both the sacrifice of Jesus and the wedding feast of heaven, in which Jesus gives us his very self—body and blood, soul and divinity.

Feet got dirty in the ancient world because people often wore sandals or went barefoot on dusty or muddy roads. The wounds in the Lord's feet, therefore, are associated with the sacraments of cleansing: *Reconciliation* (also known as Confession) and the *Anointing of the Sick*. Both of these sacraments cleanse us of sins committed after we are baptized.*

We use our **hands** to serve God and be of service to others, so these wounds represent the two sacraments of service. The right hand symbolizes the sacrament of *Holy Orders* (ordination) by which a man enters the service of God as a deacon, priest, or bishop. The left hand corresponds to the sacrament of *Marriage*, in which a couple serves each other, their children, the Church, and society. Hands are prominent in the liturgy of priestly ordination, when hands are anointed, and in the wedding ceremony, during which the couple hold hands as they exchange their vows.

That accounts for all of the visible wounds, but we still have one more sacrament to go: the sacrament of *Confirmation*. Even though we cannot see them on the corpus on the San Damiano cross, there are little wounds on Our Lord's **head** caused by the crown of thorns. We might associate these head wounds with the crowning sacrament of Confirmation, when a person's head is anointed by a bishop or his appointed representative. Confirmation is also the sacrament that conforms us to Jesus as Head of the Church, sharing in his threefold office of Priest, Prophet, and King.

Everybody knows what they're supposed to do when approaching a stop sign, but the sign itself does not make people stop—and some drivers hardly slow down. A road sign is merely an indicator, a symbol. A sacrament, on the other hand, actually causes what it symbolizes. Baptism, for example, not only symbolizes spiritual cleansing and rebirth into the Church, but it also makes spiritual cleansing and rebirth a reality within a person's soul.

Real marriage, as we have seen, is based on human nature and expresses the self-giving love of a woman and a man in a lifelong union open to children. The sacrament of marriage goes beyond that by welcoming God directly into the marriage, where he strengthens the bond between the spouses by infusing it with his own faithfulness. This is not merely symbolic. It is a

*It is highly recommended that Catholic Christians make use of the sacrament of Reconciliation before the wedding. No bride, and pretty much no groom, would forget to take a shower before they walk down the aisle. But how much more important it is to allow God to cleanse the soul! The longer you have been away from Confession, the more important this is. Don't worry about any embarrassment—the priest has heard it all before. Offer your discomfort to God and concentrate on the liberation and the joy of leaving darkness behind and sharing in the sacrament of Marriage with a pure heart. Drink from this fountain of life.

real and powerful grace. The spouses, of course, must continue to invite God into their lives, especially by taking advantage of the blessings of Confession and participation in the Sunday Eucharist, and also by prayer and service to others. If they do this, God's sacramental presence in their marriage will help them to heal the wounds of selfishness and develop the virtues they need to live out the meaning of marriage in a beautiful and liberating way.

Sacramental marriage and the two greatest mysteries

When Moses approached God in the burning bush on Mt. Sinai, God told him to remove his sandals because Moses was standing on holy ground. Well, this might be a good time for us to kick off our shoes, because we are coming, via marriage, to the two deepest mysteries of all: the Trinity and the mission of Jesus. Sacramental marriage, as we have seen, is a fountain of divine life, leading us to Jesus, who in turn leads us to the source of life, which is the Trinity. The Trinity is mysteriously present in the love of husband and wife and child. This earthly love prepares us to share in the divine love we partake of in the Eucharist. And it prepares us for the great wedding feast of heaven.

The Person and mission of Jesus

Many illustrious people have dedicated their lives to a mission. Mahatma Gandhi, for example, was devoted to achieving autonomy for the people of India, and Martin Luther King Jr. gave his life for the cause of securing equal rights for African Americans. Jesus also has a mission: to reconcile fallen human beings with God. However, not only does Jesus *have* a mission—he *is* his mission. Both human and divine, he is himself the perfect reconciliation of each one of us with God. He is what he has come to do. His mission is so personal and intimate that it is often referred to as a marriage, a marriage of God and his people in which we are raised up to share in the life and love of God. God uses human marriage to both reflect and assist with this reconciliation.

The ultimate fountain of life: The Trinity

The Trinity is the ultimate mystery, revealing that God is one and also a community of love—Father, Son, and Holy Spirit. Using the chart on page 99, let's examine the remarkable connections among three realms—the realm of the Blessed Trinity, from which comes the realm of Jesus and the Church, out of which issues the realm of marriage and family life.

It starts with the *Father*. Before the beginning of time, he makes a complete gift of himself, of all that he is. This gift is the *Son*. The Son receives his being from the Father and, in infinite gratitude, gives himself back to the Father. The love between the Father and the Son is so full of divine life that it is not merely some energy or force but rather a divine Person, the *Holy*

Spirit, who comes from, witnesses, and by his very being proclaims the love between the Father and the Son.

Jesus and his Bride, the Church

It is the Father's will to share existence with his Creation, which he calls into being through the Son and with the Holy Spirit. When the human race falls into disobedience, the Father sends his own Son as Savior. Jesus, without ceasing to be the Second Person of the Trinity, takes up and thereby elevates a human nature, becoming like us in all things except sin. In obedience to his Father, Jesus makes a complete gift of himself to his Bride, the Church. He pours himself out for his Bride, especially on the Cross—and in the Eucharist. The Church receives her very being as a community of love from this self-gift of Jesus, and in gratitude she makes a complete gift of herself to him in return. From the union of Jesus and his Church, through the waters of baptism, the people of God are born. That's us! As Christians, we come from, witness, and by our very being proclaim the love between Christ and his Church.

Marriage and family

The third realm is marriage and family life. The Church prepares a young man to be a responsible husband and father, and a young woman to be a responsible wife and mother. The husband promises a complete gift of himself to his wife in their wedding vows, and he ratifies this gift with his whole body and soul in marital intercourse. The wife fully participates in the promise of the vows and in the consummation in the marriage bed. She receives the gift that is her husband and gives herself back completely to him. This mutual self-giving is so full of goodness that it overflows with love and life and inspires the couple to give thanks through prayer and service to others. Sometimes this union of husband and wife is crowned with the creation of a brand new human being, called to eternal life. That child comes from, witnesses, and by its very being proclaims the love between his or her mom and dad. By the act of marital intercourse, husband and wife have become one flesh. This process is finalized in the conception, birth, and education of a child, who will embody their love forever.

We can see how life and love come forth from the Trinity to bear fruit in the Church and then in the family. The family brings its members—along with as many other people as possible—into the life of the Church, and the Church brings them all into the life of the Trinity and the great wedding feast of heaven. Marriage and family life therefore participate in both the communion of Persons of the Trinity and the sacrificial love of Jesus for his Bride, the Church. The interaction of these two mysteries defines the nature of sacramental marriage. Let's look at them a little more closely.

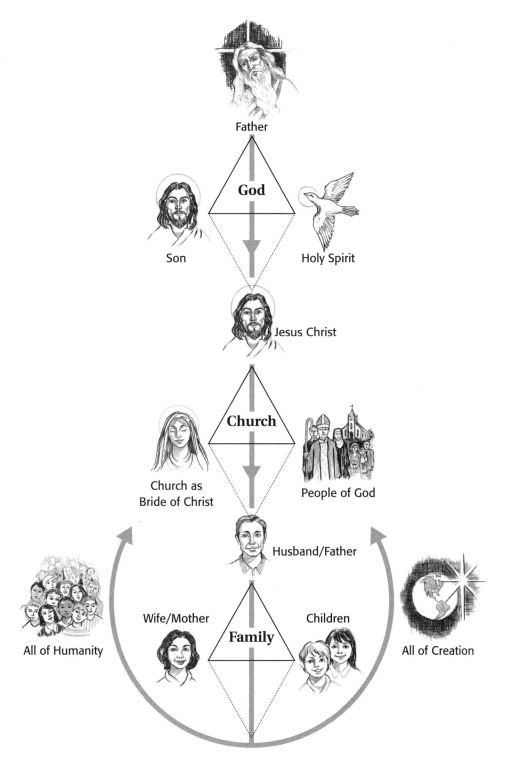

Father

God

Son

Holy Spirit

Jesus Christ

Church

Church as
Bride of Christ

People of God

Husband/Father

All of Humanity

Wife/Mother

Family

Children

All of Creation

Sacrificial forgiveness

Christ gave himself on the Cross for his Bride in order to save her from sin and to make her his helper in the great work of salvation. What Christ did for the Church, husbands and wives must do for each other in union with Christ. Husbands and wives must practice a heroic forgiveness—but also avoid the doormat kind. I knew a mother, for example, who readily forgave her teenage children their frequent disrespect, but this was doormat forgiveness because she did not hold the kids accountable for their behavior. Such forgiveness can be interpreted as an invitation to "wipe your feet here."

Heroic forgiveness, on the other hand, forgives generously but also employs the virtue of prudence to appropriately hold people responsible for their actions. In this way, husband and wife share in the forgiveness of Christ, grounded in the humility and security of a child of God. They are honest about their own faults, and their confidence in God's love helps them through the most rugged terrain. They may struggle to reach the goal of heroic forgiveness, but grace gives them the capacity, nevertheless, to call forth the best in another person and to always remember the irreplaceable value of the transgressing wife, husband, or child. This helps both the one forgiven and the one forgiving to become more like God.

Marriage, like the celibacy embraced by some for the sake of the kingdom of God, is a way of the cross. There is a reciprocal inequality in which spouses take turns giving themselves up for the good of the other. Though husband and wife are equal in dignity, they experience this reciprocal inequality as they make sacrifices and forgive each other. Through this, each spouse is perfected in love and prepared for the Kingdom of God.

Steps in the Healing Process[1]	
Physical Wound	**Spiritual Wound**
Remove arrow or other cause	Remove cause of injustice (as much as possible)
Cleanse wound	Cleanse wound by setting aside vengeance
Apply antibiotic ointment and bandage	Seek God's healing grace and love
Repeat daily as long as needed	Repeat daily as long as needed
Learn to live with the scar until the final resurrection	Learn to live with the scar until the final resurrection

Communion: The Trinity in marriage and family life

The marital way of the Cross, paradoxically, leads to the greatest joy. Through forgiveness and mutual self-sacrifice, the spouses may experience, even in this life, at least fleeting moments of transcendent intimacy, union, and peace that reflect something of the joy of the Trinity. The love of the family is infused, as it were, with the prayerful love of the Church, which is infused with the absolute love of the Trinity. This community of love enables each member of the family to become the unique person that God intends him or her to be. As St. Athanasius said, "God became human so that humans might become gods."[2] Of course, St. Athanasius does not mean independent, pagan-style gods, but he uses intentionally shocking language to describe what is beyond words: human persons who have come to participate in the life and love of the One True God.

It is the nature of sacramental marriage, therefore, to alternate between the works of sacrificial forgiveness on the one hand and the joy of communion on the other. Each spouse, in a sense, becomes Christ on the Cross for the other. Communion, on the other hand, is all about a mutual sharing in God's infinite love, which swallows up all the pain and leaves only joy.

In Christian marriage, the spouses, in union with Christ, help each other and their children to share ever more fully in divine life. It doesn't get better than this until heaven, when we shall see God as he is and mysteriously become more like him (see 1 John 3:2b).

Mary and the wedding feast in Cana

Imagine a joyous wedding in ancient Israel, with the whole village gathered in their festal garments, ready for a couple of days of serious partying. But, in an unheard-of gaffe, the supply of wine runs dry. This catastrophe is exactly what happened spiritually to our first parents, Adam and Eve. They were celebrating their marriage to each other and their spiritual marriage to God, but the wine of divine joy evaporated. In their case, it was because they had rebelled against God.

Many long and sorrowful centuries later, at a wedding feast in the village of Cana, God created the "coincidence" of the lack of physical wine. Why? So that Mary, the Mother of Jesus, would have occasion to bring her son's attention to this lack and its spiritual significance as alienation from God. She knows that her beloved son will have to suffer much physically and spiritually to restore us to the joy of communion with God. And so it is a great sacrifice for her to tell Jesus the physical and spiritual truth: "They have no wine" (John 2:3). But she also knows that it is the Father's will to bring this ultimate joy of the spirit to those who are willing to accept it.

Mary is the New Eve, by God's grace made a suitable helper for Jesus, the New Adam. She instructs the servers, "Do whatever he tells you" (John 2:5). She is still teaching us the same thing today: "Do whatever he tells you." She is still interceding for us with her Son, still seeking to restore for us—through his sacrifice—the wine of divine joy in our marriages and in our relationships with God. With the help of her prayers, may the good waters of human love be transformed for you into the delicious wine of eternal life.

Creating Your Love Story

1. Do you think marriage is about helping each other more to earthly happiness or to eternal happiness? What difference does it make in your marriage if your primary goal is earthly or if it is heavenly?

2. How good is each of you at forgiving in a way that is loving and healing for everyone involved? What can you do to improve in this area?

3. Jesus raised marriage to the exalted status of a sacrament, in which he makes present his death and resurrection. What do baptism, and the other sacraments you may have received, mean to each of you?

4. If your love as husband and wife is to reflect the love of God and his Son, Jesus, what things might you do to show this love to each other in your day-to-day lives?

Live Your Story of Love

THROUGHOUT HISTORY, YOUNG PEOPLE, testing their capacity for love, have been susceptible to overblown romanticism. They are inclined to exalt love, to overestimate the perfections of their beloved, and to underestimate their own weaknesses. Adults, on the other hand, have inevitably discovered more than a few times the sad fact of weakness—their own and others'. These hard lessons in reality can lead either to cynicism or to wisdom. Cynicism dissolves the youthful dream of love down to the hard remnant of lust, money, and power. Wisdom, however, recognizes in youthful fantasy a glimpse of a love that, in reality, vastly exceeds the dream.

Shakespeare's comedic love story *Romeo and Juliet* turns into a tragedy because the adults, with the exception of Friar Lawrence, have bought into a cynical view of love. Both the Montague and Capulet families are steeped not in kindness and friendship but in pride and revenge. The elders, blinded by selfishness, prove to be far more foolish than the young lovers—and their folly creates a culture of death that ensnares the young.

What does this have to do with *your* love story? The tragedy of our times is that it is so easy for couples to get trapped by the pleasures and minimal commitments of our cynical, consumerist society, which is at least as foolish as the society of Renaissance Verona in Shakespeare's comedy-turned-trage-dy. On the other hand, with an understanding of the teachings of Christ and his Church about marriage, you can write your love story in the context of

God's love story. You can reveal God's love to each other in your human love. Your mutual love can lead others, including your children, to a strong human love and can even point them to divine love.

The second time Romeo encounters Juliet, she appears suddenly on a balcony above. He enthuses, "But, soft! what light through yonder window breaks? It is the east, and Juliet is the sun." This is heady stuff. The sun is a symbol of divinity, and Romeo's words effectively equate Juliet with God. Later in the same scene, Juliet calls Romeo "the god of my idolatry."[1] This may be charming poetry, but it is a dream out of touch with the facts, and the dreamer is subject to a rude awakening.

The lovers soon encounter reality in all of its harshness, but they are ennobled as they strive to be faithful in the face of mounting difficulties. They rise above the prejudice and hatred of their elders, and in the end, their marriage becomes an icon of love for the supposed grownups and for all of us as well. Along with Romeo, we learn the liberating truth that, while Juliet is *not* the sun, which is the source of its own light, she *is* created to be like a clean window through which the light of God can shine. Human love is made to lead to divine love, and divine love purifies and elevates human love.

Your own love story is connected to all the other love stories in the world, and especially with the love story of God and his people, of Jesus and his Bride, the Church. Each one of you is unique, unrepeatable, and irreplaceable, and therefore your relationship with your spouse is unique. The two of you now have the chance to write—with the ink of thoughts, words, and deeds, with the very substance of your lives—your own love story in the context of God's love story. Make that love story a total gift of self, of all you are meant to be. Make it beautiful and make it deep. Make it true and make it strong. Make it forever and make it generous in the service of life.

But, soft! what light through yonder window shines? It is the light of Christ. Let it come through, and it will illuminate both the challenge and the nobility of love, human and divine.

What happened in Cana 2,000 years ago happens today at every wedding celebration: that which makes your wedding full and profoundly true will be the presence of the Lord who reveals himself and gives his grace. It is his presence that offers the "good wine"; he is the secret to full joy, that which truly warms the heart. It is the presence of Jesus at the celebration. May it be a beautiful celebration, but with Jesus! Not with a worldly spirit, no! You can feel it when the Lord is there.[1]

—Pope Francis

The Order of Celebrating Matrimony and Readings

The code numbers for the readings (i.e., A-1, B-1, etc.) correspond to The Order of Celebrating Matrimony Ritual Cards published by Ave Maria Press, Notre Dame, Indiana 46556. The numbers in parentheses refer to the Lectionary numbers when appropriate.

THE ORDER FOR CELEBRATING MATRIMONY WITHIN MASS

Introductory Rites

Entrance Rite
Greeting

Afterwards the priest, with hands joined, sings or says:
   Let us pray.

Opening Prayer

*Priest and people pray silently for a while. Then the priest extends his hands
and sings or says the opening prayer, at the end of which the people respond:*
   Amen.

   We have come rejoicing into the house of the Lord
   for this celebration, dear brothers and sisters,
   and now we stand with N. and N.
   on the day they intend to form a home of their own.
   For them this is a moment of unique importance.
   So let us support them
   with our affection,
   with our friendship,
   and with our prayer as their brothers and sisters.
   Let us listen attentively with them
   to the word that God speaks to us today.
   Then, with holy Church,
   let us humbly pray to God the Father,
   through Christ our Lord,
   for this couple, his servants,
   that he lovingly accept them,
   bless them,
   and make them always one.
   R. **Amen.**

   or

   N. and N., the Church shares your joy
   and warmly welcomes you,

together with your families and friends,
as today,
in the presence of God our Father,
you establish between yourselves
a lifelong partnership.
May the Lord hear you on this your joyful day.
May he send you help from heaven and protect you.
May he grant you your hearts' desire
and fulfill every one of your prayers.
R. **Amen.**

Penitential Rite is omitted.
Gloria

Liturgy of the Word

Note: These readings are taken from the Lectionary for Mass.
* Ave Maria Press Ritual Card number / ** Lectionary number

Old Testament Reading

B-1* / 801-1**
Genesis 1:26–28, 31a
Male and female he created them

A reading from the Book of Genesis
Then God said:
"Let us make man in our image, after our likeness.
Let them have dominion over the fish of the sea,
    the birds of the air, and the cattle,
    and over all the wild animals
    and all the creatures that crawl on the ground."

God created man in his image;
    in the image of God he created him;
    male and female he created them.

God blessed them, saying:
    "Be fertile and multiply;
    fill the earth and subdue it.

Have dominion over the fish of the sea, the birds of the air,
    and all the living things that move on the earth."
God looked at everything he had made, and he found it very good.
The word of the Lord.

B-2* / 801-2**
Genesis 2:18–24
The two of them become one body.

A reading from the Book of Genesis
The Lord God said: "It is not good for the man to be alone.
I will make a suitable partner for him."
So the Lord God formed out of the ground
    various wild animals and various birds of the air,
    and he brought them to the man to see what he would call them;
    whatever the man called each of them would be its name.
The man gave names to all the cattle,
    all the birds of the air, and all wild animals;
    but none proved to be the suitable partner for the man.

So the Lord God cast a deep sleep on the man,
    and while he was asleep,
    he took one of his ribs and closed up its place with flesh.
The Lord God then built up into a woman the rib
    that he had taken from the man.
When he brought her to the man, the man said:

    "This one, at last, is bone of my bones
        and flesh of my flesh;
    This one shall be called 'woman',
        for out of 'her man' this one has been taken."

That is why a man leaves his father and mother
    and clings to his wife,
    and the two of them become one body.
The word of the Lord.

B-3* / 801-3**
Genesis 24:48–51, 58–67
In his love for Rebekah, Isaac found solace after the death of his mother.

A reading from the Book of Genesis
The servant of Abrahm said to Laban:
"I bowed down in worship to the Lord,
blessing the Lord, the god of my master Abraham,
who had led me on the right road
to obtain the daughter of my master's kinsman for his son.
If, therefore, you have in mind to show true loyalty to my master,
let me know:
but if not, let me know that, too.
I can then proceed accordingly."

Laban and his household said in reply:
"This thing comes from the Lord;
we can say nothing to you either for or against it.
Here is Rebekah, ready for you;
take her with you,
that she may become the wife of your master's son,
as the Lord has said."

So they called Rebekah and asked her,
"Do you wish to go with this man?"
She answered, "I do."
At this they allowed their sister Rebekah and her nurse to take leave,
along with Abraham's servant and his men.
Invoking a blessing on Rebekah, they said;

"Sister, may you grow
into thousands of myriads;
And may your descendants gain possession
of the gates of their enemies!"

Then Rebekah and her maids started out;
they mounted their camels and followed the man.
So the servant took Rebekah and went on his way.

Meanwhile Isaac had gone from Beer-lahai-roi
and was living in the region of the Negeb.

One day toward evening he went out . . . in the field,
>and as he looked around, he noticed that camels were approaching.
>Rebekah, too, was looking about, and when she saw him,
>she alighted from her camel and asked the servant,
>"Who is the man out there, walking through the fields toward us?"
"That is my master," replied the servant.
Then she covered herself with her veil.

The servant recounted to Isaac all the things he had done.
Then Isaac took Rebekah into his tent;
>he married her, and thus she became his wife.
In his love for her, Isaac found solace
>after the death of his mother Sarah.
The word of the Lord.

B-4* / 801-4**
Tobit 7:6–14
May the Lord of heaven prosper you both. May he grant you mercy and peace.

A reading from the Book of Tobit
Raphael and Tobiah entered the house of Raguel and greeted him.
Raguel sprang up and kissed Tobiah , shedding tears of joy.
But when he heard that Tobit had lost his eyesight,
>he was grieved and wept aloud.
He said to Tobiah:
>"My child, God bless you!
You are the son of a noble and good father.
But what a terrible misfortune
>that such a righteous and charitable man
>should be afflicted with blindness!"
He continued to weep in the arms of his kinsman Tobiah.
His wife Edna also wept for Tobit;
>and even their daughter Sarah began to weep.

Afterward, Raguel slaughtered a ram from the flock
>and gave them a cordial reception.
When they had bathed and reclined to eat,
>Tobiah said to Raphael, "Brother Azariah,
>ask Raguel to let me marry my kinswoman Sarah."

Raguel overheard the words;
>so he said to the boy:
"Eat and drink and be merry tonight,
>for no man is more entitled to marry my daughter Sarah
>than you, brother.
Besides, not even I have the right to give her to anyone but you,
>because you are my closest relative.
But I will explain the situation to you very frankly.
I have given her in marriage to seven men,
>all of whom were kinsmen of ours,
>and all died on the very night they approached her.
But now, son, eat and drink.
I am sure the Lord will look after you both."
Tobiah answered, "I will eat or drink nothing
>until you set aside what belongs to me."

Raguel said to him: "I will do it.
She is yours according to the decree of the Book of Moses.
Your marriage to her has been decided in heaven!
Take your kinswoman;
>from now on you are her love,
>and she is your beloved.
She is yours today and ever after.
And tonight, son, may the Lord of heaven prosper you both.
May he grant you mercy and peace."
Then Raguel called his daughter Sarah, and she came to him.
He took her by the hand and gave her to Tobiah with the words:
>"Take her according to the law.
According to the decree written in the Book of Moses she is your wife.
Take her and bring her back safely to your father.
And may the God of heaven grant both of you peace and prosperity."
He then called her mother and told her to bring a scroll,
>so that he might draw up a marriage contract
>stating that he gave Sarah to Tobiah as his wife
>according to the decree of the Mosaic law.
Her mother brought the scroll,
>and he drew up the contact,
>to which they affixed their seals.

Afterward they began to eat and drink.
The word of the Lord.

B-5* / 801-5**
Tobit 8:4b–8
Allow us to live together to a happy old age.

A reading from the Book of Tobit
On their wedding night Tobiah arose from bed and said to his wife,
    "Sister, get up. Let us pray and beg our Lord
    to have mercy on us and to grant us deliverance."
Sarah got up, and they started to pray
    and beg that deliverance might be theirs.
They began with these words:

    "Blessed are you, O God of our fathers;
        praised be your name forever and ever.
    Let the heavens and all your creation
        praise you forever.
    You made Adam and you gave him his wife Eve
        to be his help and support;
        and from these two the human race descended.
    You said, "It is not good for the man to be alone;
        let us make him a partner like himself.'
    Now, Lord, you know that I take this wife of mine
        not because of lust,
        but for a noble purpose.
    Call down your mercy on me and on her,
        and allow us to live together to a happy old age."

They said together, "Amen, amen."
The word of the Lord.

B-6* / 801-6**
Proverbs 31:10–13, 19–20, 30–31
The woman who fears the Lord is to be praised.

A reading from the Book of Proverbs
When one finds a worthy wife,
    her value is far beyond pearls.
Her husband, entrusting his heart to her,
    has an unfailing prize.
She brings him good, and not evil
    all the days of her life.

She obtains wool and flax
>and makes cloth with skillful hands.
She puts her hands to the distaff,
>and her fingers ply the spindle.
She reaches out her hands to the poor,
>and extends her arms to the needy.
Charm is deceptive and beauty fleeting;
>the woman who fears the Lord is to be praised.
Give her a reward of her labors,
>and let her works praise her at the city gates.
The word of the Lord.

B-7* / 801-7**
Song of Songs 2:8–10, 14, 16a; 8:6–7a
Stern as death is love.

A reading from the Song of Songs
Hark! My lover — here he comes
>springing across the mountains,
>leaping across the hills.
My lover is like a gazelle
>or a young stag.
Here he stands behind our wall,
>gazing through the windows,
>peering through the lattices.
My lover speaks; he says to me,
>"Arise, my beloved, my dove, my beautiful one, and come!

"O my dove in the clefts of the rock,
>in the secret recesses of the cliff,
Let me see you,
>let me hear your voice,
For your voice is sweet,
>and you are lovely."

My lover belongs to me and I to him.
>He says to me:

"Set me as a seal on your heart,
>as a seal on your arm;
For stern as death is love,

relentless as the nether-world is devotion;
    its flames are a blazing fire.
Deep waters cannot quench love,
    nor floods sweep it away."
The word of the Lord.

B-8* / 801-8**
Sirach 26: 1–4, 13–16 (Vg. 26: 1–4, 16–21)
Like the sun rising in the Lord's heavens, the beauty of a virtuous wife is the radiance of her home.

A reading from the Book of Sirach
Blessed the husband of a good wife,
    twice lengthened are his days;
A worthy wife brings joy to her husband,
    peaceful and full is his life.
A good wife is a generous gift
    bestowed upon him who fears the Lord;
Be he rich or poor, his heart is content,
    and a smile is ever on his face.

A gracious wife delights her husband,
    her thoughtfulness puts flesh on his bones;
A gift from the Lord is her governed speech,
    and her firm virtue is of surpassing worth.
Choicest of blessings is a modest wife,
    priceless her chaste soul.
A holy and decent woman adds grace upon grace;
    indeed, no price is worthy of her temperate soul.
Like the sun rising in the Lord's heavens,
    the beauty of a virtuous wife is the radiance of her home.
The word of the Lord.

B-9* / 801-9**
Jeremiah 31:31–32a, 33–34a
I will make a new covenant with the house of Israel and the house of Judah.

A reading from the Book of the Prophet Jeremiah
The days are coming, says the Lord,
    when I will make a new covenant with the house of Israel

and the house of Judah.
It will not be like the covenant I made with their fathers:
    the day I took them by the hand
    to lead them forth from the land of Egypt.
But this is the covenant which I will make
    with the house of Israel after those days, says the LORD.
I will place my law within them, and write it upon their hearts;
    I will be their God, and they shall be my people.
No longer will they have need to teach their friends and relatives
    how to know the LORD.
All, from least to greatest, shall know me, says the LORD.
The word of the Lord.

Responsorial Psalm

C-1* / 803-1**
Psalm 33:12 and 18, 20–21, 22

R. (5b) The earth is full of the goodness of the Lord.
Blessed the nation whose God is the LORD,
    the people he has chosen as his heritage.
Yes, those who fear him,
    who hope in his merciful love.
R. The earth is full of the goodness of the Lord.
Our soul is waiting for the LORD,
    He is our help and our shield.
In him do our hearts find joy.
    We trust in his holy name.
R. The earth is full of the goodness of the Lord.
May your merciful love be upon us,
    as we hope in you, O LORD.
R. The earth is full of the goodness of the Lord.

C-2* / 803-2**
Psalm 34:2–3, 4–5, 6–7, 8–9

R. (2a) I will bless the Lord at all times.
Or: *R.* (9a) Taste and see the goodness of the Lord.
I will bless the LORD at all times,
    praise of him is always in my mouth.

In the LORD my soul shall make its boast;
 the humble shall hear and be glad.
R. **I will bless the Lord at all times.**
Or: *R.* Taste and see the goodness of the Lord.
Glorify the LORD with me;
 together let us praise his name.
I sought the LORD, and he answered me;
 from all my terrors he set me free.
R. **I will bless the Lord at all times.**
Or: *R.* Taste and see the goodness of the Lord.
Look toward him and be radiant;
 let your faces not be abashed.
This lowly one called; the LORD heard,
 and rescued him from all his distress.
R. **I will bless the Lord at all times.**
Or: *R.* Taste and see the goodness of the Lord.
The angel of the LORD is encamped
 around those who fear him, to rescue them.
Taste and see that the LORD is good.
 Blessed the man who seeks refuge in him.
R. **I will bless the Lord at all times.**
Or: *R.* Taste and see the goodness of the Lord.

C-3* / 803-3**
Psalm 103:1–2, 8 and 13, 17–18a

R. **(8a) The Lord is kind and merciful.**
Or: *R.* (see 17) The Lord's kindness is everlasting to those who fear him.
Bless the LORD, O my soul,
 and all within me, his holy name.
Bless the LORD, O my soul,
 and never forget all his benefits.
R. **The Lord is kind and merciful.**
Or: *R.* The Lord's kindness is everlasting to those who fear him.
The LORD is compassionate and gracious,
 slow to anger and rich in mercy.
As a father has compassion on his children,
 the LORD's compassion is on those who fear him.
R. **The Lord is kind and merciful.**
Or: *R.* The Lord's kindness is everlasting to those who fear him.
But the mercy of the LORD is everlasting

upon those who hold him in fear,
upon children's children his righteousness,
    for those who keep his covenant.
R. The Lord is kind and merciful.
Or: R. The Lord's kindness is everlasting to those who fear him.

C-4* / 803-4**
Psalm 112:1bc–2, 3–4, 5–7a, 7b–8, 9

R. (see 1) Blessed the man who greatly delights in the Lord's commands.
Or: R. Alleluia.
Blessed the man who fears the LORD,
    who takes great delight in his commandments.
His descendants shall be powerful on earth;
    the generation of the upright will be blest.
R. Blessed the man who greatly delights in the Lord's commands.
Or: R. Alleluia.
Riches and wealth are in his house;
    his righteousness stands firm forever.
A light rises in the darkness for the upright;
    he is generous, merciful, and righteous.
R. Blessed the man who greatly delights in the Lord's commands.
Or: R. Alleluia.
It goes well for the man who deals generously and lends,
    who conducts his affairs with justice.
He will never be moved;
    forever shall the righteous be remembered.
He has no fear of evil news.
R. Blessed the man who greatly delights in the Lord's commands.
Or: R. Alleluia.
With a firm heart, he trusts in the LORD.
With a steadfast heart he shall not fear;
    he will see the downfall of his foes.
R. Blessed the man who greatly delights in the Lord's commands.
Or: R. Alleluia.
Openhanded, he gives to the poor;
    his righteousness stands firm forever.
    His might shall be exalted in glory.
R. Blessed the man who greatly delights in the Lord's commands.
Or: R. Alleluia.

C-5* / 803-5**
Psalm 128:1–2, 3, 4–5ac and 6a

R. (see 1a) Blessed are those who fear the Lord.
Or: *R.* (4) See how the Lord blesses those who fear him.
Blessed are all who fear the LORD,
    and walk in his ways!
By the labor of your hands you shall eat.
    You will be blessed and prosper.
R. Blessed are those who fear the Lord.
Or: *R.* See how the Lord blesses those who fear him.
Your wife like a fruitful vine
    in the heart of your house;
your children like shoots of the olive
    around your table.
R. Blessed are those who fear the Lord.
Or: *R.* See how the Lord blesses those who fear him.
Indeed thus shall be blessed
    the man who fears the LORD.
May the LORD bless you from Zion
    all the days of your life!
      May you see your children's children.
R. Blessed are those who fear the Lord.
Or: *R.* See how the Lord blesses those who fear him.

C-6* / 803-6**
Psalm 145:8–9, 10 and 15, 17–18

R. (9a) How good is the Lord to all.
The LORD is kind and full of compassion,
    slow to anger, abounding in mercy.
How good is the LORD to all,
    compassionate to all his creatures.
R. How good is the Lord to all.
All your works shall thank you, O LORD,
    and all your faithful ones bless you.
The eyes of all look to you
    and you give them their food in due season.
R. How good is the Lord to all.
The LORD is righteous in all his ways,

and holy in all his deeds.
The LORD is close to all who call him,
    who call on him in truth.
R. How good is the Lord to all.

C-7* / 803-7**
Psalm 148:1–2, 3–4, 9–10, 11–13a, 13c–14a

  R. **(13a) Let all praise the name of the Lord.**
Or: *R.* **Alleluia.**
Praise the LORD from the heavens;
    praise him in the heights.
Praise him, all his angels;
    praise him, all his hosts.
R. **Let all praise the name of the Lord.**
Or: *R.* **Alleluia.**
Praise him, sun and moon;
    praise him, all shining stars.
Praise him, highest heavens,
    and the waters above the heavens.
R. **Let all praise the name of the Lord.**
Or: *R.* **Alleluia.**
Mountains and all hills,
    fruit trees and all cedars,
beasts, both wild and tame,
    creeping things and birds on the wing.
R. **Let all praise the name of the Lord.**
Or: *R.* **Alleluia.**
Kings of the earth and all peoples,
    princes and all judges of the earth,
young men and maidens as well,
    the old and the young together.
Let them praise the name of the LORD,
    for his name alone is exalted.
R. **Let all praise the name of the Lord.**
Or: *R.* **Alleluia.**
His splendor above heaven and earth.
    He exalts the strength of his people.
R. **Let all praise the name of the Lord.**
Or: *R.* **Alleluia.**

New Testament Reading

D-1* / 802-1**
Romans 8:31b–35, 37–39
What will separate us from the love of Christ?

    A reading from the Letter of Saint Paul to the Romans
    Brothers and sisters:
    If God is for us, who can be against us?
    He did not spare his own Son
        but handed him over for us all,
        will he not also give us everything else along with him?
    It is God who acquits us.
    Who will condemn?
    It is Christ Jesus who died, rather, was raised,
        who also is at the right hand of God,
        who indeed intercedes for us.
    What will separate us from the love of Christ?
    Will anguish, or distress, or persecution, or famine,
        or nakedness, or peril, or the sword?
    No, in all these things, we conquer overwhelmingly
        through him who loved us.
    For I am convinced that neither death, nor life,
        nor angels, nor principalities,
        nor present things, nor future things,
        nor powers, nor height, nor depth,
        nor any other creature will be able to separate us
        from the love of God in Christ Jesus our LORD.
    The word of the Lord.

D-2* / 802-2**
Long Form: Romans 12: 1–2, 9–18
Offer your bodies as a living sacrifice, holy and pleasing to God.

    A reading from the Letter of Saint Paul to the Romans
    I urge you, brothers and sisters, by the mercies of God,
        to offer bodies as a living sacrifice,
        holy and pleasing to God, your spiritual worship.
    Do not conform yourselves to this age
        but be transformed by the renewal of your mind,

that you may discern what is the will of God,
what is good and pleasing and perfect.

Let love be sincere;
   hate what is evil,
   hold on to what is good;
   love one another with mutual affection;
   anticipate one another in showing honor.
Do not grow slack in zeal,
   be fervent in spirit,
   serve the Lord.
Rejoice in hope,
   endure in affliction,
   persevere in prayer.
Contribute to the needs of the holy ones,
   exercise hospitality.
Bless those who persecute you,
   bless and do not curse them.
Rejoice with those who rejoice,
   weep with those who weep.
Have the same regard for one another;
   do not be haughty but associate with the lowly;
   do not be wise in your own estimation.
Do not repay anyone evil for evil;
   be concerned for what is noble in the sight of all.
If possible, on your part, live at peace with all.
The word of the Lord.

or

Short Form: Romans 12:1–2, 9–13
Offer your bodies as a living sacrifice, holy and pleasing to God.

A reading from the Letter of Saint Paul to the Romans
I urge you, brothers and sisters, by the mercies of God,
   to offer your bodies as a living sacrifice,
   holy and pleasing to God, your spiritual worship.
Do not conform yourselves to this age
   but be transformed by the renewal of your mind,
   that you may discern what is the will of God,
   what is good and pleasing and perfect.

Let love be sincere;
>   hate what is evil,
>   hold on to what is good;
>   love one another with mutual affection;
>   anticipate one another in showing honor.
Do not grow slack in zeal,
>   be fervent in spirit,
>   serve the Lord.
Rejoice in hope,
>   endure in affliction,
>   persevere in prayer.
Contribute to the needs of the holy ones,
>   exercise hospitality.
The word of the Lord.

D-3* / 802-3**
Romans 15: 1b–3a, 5–7, 13
Welcome one another as Christ welcomed you.

A reading from the Letter of Saint Paul to the Romans
Brothers and sisters:
We ought to put up with the failings of the weak and not to
please ourselves;
>   let each of us please our neighbor for the good,
>   for building up.
For Christ did not please himself.
May the God of endurance and encouragement
>   grant you to think in harmony with one another,
>   in keeping with Christ Jesus,
>   that with one accord you may with one voice
>   glorify the God and Father of our Lord Jesus Christ.

Welcome one another, then, as Christ welcomed you,
>   for the glory of God.
May the God of hope fill you with all joy and peace in believing,
>   so that you may abound in hope by the power of the Holy Spirit.
The word of the Lord.

D-4* / 802-4**
1 Corinthians 6:13c–15a, 17–20
Your body is a temple of the Spirit.

A reading from the first letter of Saint Paul to the Corinthians
Brothers and sisters:
The body is not for immorality, but for the Lord,
   and the Lord is for the body;
   God raised the Lord and will also raise us by his power.

Do you not know that your bodies are members of Christ?
Whoever is joined to the Lord becomes one spirit with him.
Avoid immorality.
Every other sin a person commits is outside the body,
   but the immoral person sins against his own body.
Do you not know that your body
   is a temple of the Holy Spirit within you,
   whom you have from God, and that you are not your own?
For you have been purchased at a price.
Therefore glorify God in your body.
The word of the Lord.

D-5* / 802-5**
1 Corinthians 12:31–13:8a
If I do not have love, I gain nothing.

A reading from the first Letter of Saint Paul to the Corinthians.
Brothers and sisters:
Strive eagerly for the greatest spiritual gifts.

But I shall show you a still more excellent way.

If I speak in human and angelic tongues
   but do not have love,
   I am a resounding gong or a clashing cymbal.
And if I have the gift of prophecy
   and comprehend all mysteries and all knowledge;
   if I have all faith so as to move mountains,
   but do not have love, I am nothing.
If I give away everything I own,

and I hand my body over so that I may boast
but do not have love, I gain nothing.

Love is patient, love is kind.
It is not jealous, is not pompous
    it is not inflated, it is not rude,
    it does not seek its own interests,
    it is not quick-tempered, it does not brood over injury,
       it does not rejoice over wrongdoing
    but rejoices with the truth.
It bears all things, believes all things,
    hopes all things, endures all things.
Love never fails.
The word of the Lord.

D-6# / 807-2**
Ephesians 4:1–6
One Body and one Spirit.

A readings from the Letter of Saint Paul to the Ephesians
Brothers and sisters:
I, a prisoner for the LORD,
    urge you to live in a matter worthy of the call you have received,
    with all humility and gentleness, with patience,
    bearing with one another through love,
    striving to preserve the unity of the Spirit
    through the bond of peace: one Body and one Spirit,
    as you were also called to the one hope of your call;
    one LORD, one faith, one baptism;
    one God and Father of all,
    who is over all and through all and in all.
The word of the Lord.

D-7* / 802-6**
Long form: Ephesians 5:2a, 21–33
This is a great mystery, but I speak in reference to Christ and the Church.

A reading from the Letter of Saint Paul to the Ephesians
Brothers and sisters:
Live in love, as Christ loved us
    and handed himself over for us.

Be subordinate to one another out of reverence for Christ.
Wives should be subordinate to their husbands as to the LORD.
For the husband is head of his wife
 just as Christ is head of the Church,
 he himself the savior of the body.
As the Church is subordinate to Christ,
 so wives should be subordinate to their husbands in everything.
Husbands, love your wives
 even as Christ loved the Church
 and handed himself over for her to sanctify her,
 cleansing her by the bath of water with the word,
 that he might present to himself the church in splendor,
 without spot or wrinkle or any such thing,
 that she might be holy and without blemish.
So also husbands should love their wives as their own bodies.
He who loves his wife loves himself.
For no one hates his own flesh
 but rather nourishes and cherishes it,
 even as Christ does the Church,
 because we are members of his Body.

For this reason a man shall leave his father and his mother
 and be joined to his wife,
and the two shall become one flesh.

This is a great mystery,
 but I speak in reference to Christ and the Church.
In any case, each one of you should love his wife as himself,
 and the wife should respect her husband.
The word of the Lord.

or

Short Form: Ephesians 5:2a, 25–32
This is a great mystery, but I speak in reference to Christ and the Church.

A reading from the Letter of Saint Paul to the Ephesians
Brothers and sisters:
Live in love, as Christ loved us
 and handed himself over to us.

Husbands, love your wives,
    even as Christ loved the Church
    and handed himself over for her to sanctify her,
    cleansing her by the bath of water with the word,
    that he might present to himself the Church in splendor,
    without spot or wrinkle or any such thing,
    that she might be holy and without blemish.
So also husbands should love their wives as their own bodies.
He who loves his wife loves himself.
For no one hates his own flesh
    but rather nourishes and cherishes it,
    even as Christ does the Church,
    because we are members of his Body.

For this reason a man shall leave his father and his mother
    and be joined to his wife,
and the two shall become one flesh.
This is a great mystery,
    but I speak in reference to Christ and the Church.
The word of the Lord.

D-8* / 802-7**
Philippians 4: 4–9
The God of peace will be with you.

A reading from the Letter of Saint Paul to the Phillippians
Brothers and sisters:
Rejoice in the Lord always.
I shall say it again: rejoice!
Your kindness should be known to all.
The Lord is near.
Have no anxiety at all, but in everything,
    by prayer and petition, with thanksgiving,
    make your requests known to God.
Then the peace of God that surpasses all understanding
    will guard your hearts and minds in Christ Jesus.

Finally, brothers and sisters,
    whatever is true, whatever is honorable,
    whatever is just, whatever is pure,
    whatever is lovely, whatever is gracious,

if there is any excellence
and if there is anything worthy of praise,
think about these things.
Keep on doing what you have learned and received
and heard and seen in me.
Then the God of peace will be with you.
The word of the Lord.

D-9* / 802-8**
Colossians 3: 12–17
And over all these put on love, that is, the bond of perfection.

A reading from the Letter of Saint Paul to the Colossians
Brothers and sisters:
Put on, as God's chosen ones, holy and beloved,
heartfelt compassion, kindness, humility, gentleness, and patience,
bearing with one another and forgiving one another,
if one has a grievance against another;
as the Lord has forgiven you, so must you also do.
And over all these put on love,
that is, the bond of perfection.
And let the peace of Christ control your hearts,
the peace into which you were also called in one Body.
And be thankful.
Let the word of Christ dwell in you richly,
as in all wisdom you teach and admonish one another,
singing psalms, hymns, and spiritual songs
with gratitude in your hearts to God.
And whatever you do, in word or in deed,
do everything in the name of the Lord Jesus,
giving thanks to God the Father through him.
The word of the Lord.

D-10* / 802-9**
Hebrews 13:1–4a, 5–6b
Let marriage be held in honor by all.

A reading from the Letter to the Hebrews
Brothers and sisters:
Let mutual love continue.

Do not neglect hospitality,
    for through it some have unknowingly entertained angels.
Be mindful of prisoners as if sharing their imprisonment,
    and of the ill-treated as of yourselves,
    for you are also in the body.
Let marriage be honored among all
    and the marriage bed be kept undefiled.
Let your life be free from love of money
    but be content with what you have,
    for he has said, *I will never forsake you or abandon you.*
Thus we may say with confidence:

The Lord is my helper,
and I will not be afraid.
The word of the Lord.

D-11* / 802-10**
1 Peter 3:1–9
Be of one mind, sympathetic, loving toward one another.

A reading from the first Letter of Saint Peter
Beloved:
You wives should be subordinate to your husbands so that,
    even if some disobey the word,
    they may be won over without a word by their wives' conduct
    when they observe your reverent and chaste behavior.
Your adornment should not be an external one:
    braiding the hair, wearing gold jewelry, or dressing in fine clothes,
    but rather the hidden character of the heart,
    expressed in the imperishable beauty
    of a gentle and calm disposition,
    which is precious in the sight of God.
For this is also how the holy women who hoped in God
    once used to adorn themselves
    and were subordinate to their husbands;
    thus Sarah obeyed Abraham calling him "lord."
You are her children when do what is good
    and fear no intimidation.

Likewise, you husbands should live with your wives in understanding,
    showing honor to the weaker female sex,

since we are joint heirs of the gift of life,
so that your prayers may not be hindered.

Finally, all of you, be of one mind, sympathetic,
loving toward one another, compassionate, humble.
Do not return evil for evil, or insult for insult;
but on the contrary, a blessing, because to this you were called,
that you might inherit a blessing.
The word of the Lord.

D-12* / 802-11**
1 John 3: 18–24
Love in deed and in truth

A reading from the first Letter of Saint John
Children, let us love not in word or speech
but in deed and truth,
Now this is how we shall know that we belong to the truth
and reassure our hearts before him
in whatever our hearts condemn,
for God is greater than our hearts and knows everything.
Beloved, if our hearts do not condemn us,
we have confidence in God
and receive from him whatever we ask,
because we keep his commandments and do what pleases him.
And his commandment is this:
we should believe in the name of his Son, Jesus Christ,
and love one another just as he commanded us.
Those who keep his commandments remain in him, and he in them,
and the way we know that he remains in us
is from the Spirit that he gave us.
The word of the Lord.

D-13* / 802-12**
1 John 4:7–12
God is love.

A reading from the first Letter of Saint John
Beloved, let us love one another,
because love is of God;
everyone who loves is begotten by God and knows God.

Whoever is without love does not know God, for God is love.
In this way the love of God was revealed to us:
    God sent his only-begotten Son into the world
    so that we might have life through him.
In this is love:
    not that we have loved God, but that he loved us
    and sent his Son as expiation for our sins.
Beloved, if God so loved us,
    we must also love one another.
No one has ever seen God.
Yet, if we love one another, God remains in us,
    and his love is brought to perfection in us.
The word of the Lord.

D-14* 802-13**
Revelation 19:1, 5–9a
Blessed are those who have been called to the wedding feast of the Lamb.

A reading from the Book of Revelation
I, John, heard what sounded like the loud voice
    of a great multitude in heaven, saying:

    "Alleluia!
Salvation, glory, and might belong to our God."

A voice coming from the throne said:

    "Praise our God, all you his servants,
        and you who revere him, small and great."

Then I heard something like the sound of a great multitude
    or the sound of rushing water or mighty peals of thunder,
    as they said:
        "Alleluia!
The Lord has established his reign,
    our God, the almighty.
Let us rejoice and be glad
    and give him glory.
For the wedding day of the Lamb has come,
    his bride has made herself ready.
She was allowed to wear

a bright, clean linen garment."
(The linen represents the righteous deeds of the holy ones.)

Then the angel said to me,
  "Write this:
  Blessed are those who have been called
  to the wedding feast of the Lamb."
The word of the Lord.

Alleluia Verse and Verse Before the Gospel

E-1* / 804-1**
1 John 4:7b

Everyone who loves is begotten of God and knows God.

E-2* / 804-2**
1 John 4:8b and 11

God is love.
Let is love one another, as God has loved us.

E-3* / 804-3**
1 John 4:12

If we love one another,
God remains in us
and his love is brought to perfection in us.

E-4* / 804-4**
1 John 4:16

Whoever remains in love,
remains in God and God in him.

Gospel

F-1* / 805-1**
Matthew 5:1–12a
Rejoice and be glad, for your reward will be great in heaven.

A reading from the holy Gospel according to Matthew
When Jesus saw the crowds, he went up the mountain,
and after he had sat down, his disciples came to him.
He began to teach them, saying:

"Blessed are the poor in spirit,
for theirs is the Kingdom of heaven.
Blessed are they who mourn,
for they will be comforted.
Blessed are the meek,
for they will inherit the land.
Blessed are they who hunger and thirst for righteousness,
for they will be satisfied.
Blessed are the merciful,
for they will be shown mercy.
Blessed are the clean of heart,
for they will see God.
Blessed are the peacemakers,
for they will be called children of God.
Blessed are they who are persecuted for the sake of righteousness,
for theirs is the Kingdom of heaven.
Blessed are you when they insult you and persecute you
and utter every kind of evil against you falsely because of me.
Rejoice and be glad,
for your reward will be great in heaven."
The Gospel of the Lord.

F-2* / 805-2**
Matthew 5:13–16
You are the light of the world.

A reading from the holy Gospel according to Matthew
Jesus said to his disciples:
"You are the salt of the earth.
But if salt loses its taste, with what can it be seasoned?
It is no longer good for anything
but to be thrown out and trampled underfoot.
You are the light of the world.
A city set on a mountain cannot be hidden.
Nor do they light a lamp and then put it under a bushel basket;
it is set on a lamp stand,

here it gives light to all in the house.
Just so, your light must shine before others,
    that they may see your good deeds
    and glorify your heavenly Father."
The Gospel of the Lord.

F-3* / 805-3**
Long Form: Matthew 7:21, 24–29
A wise man built his house on rock.

A reading form the holy Gospel according to Matthew
Jesus said to his disciples:
"Not everyone who says to me, 'Lord, Lord,'
    will enter the Kingdom of heaven,
    but only the one who does the will of my Father in heaven.

"Everyone who listens to these words of mine and acts on them
    will be like a wise man who built his house on rock.
The rain fell, the floods came,
    and the winds blew and buffeted the house.
But it did not collapse; it had been set solidly on rock.
And everyone who listens to these words of mine
    but does not act on them
    will be like a fool who built his house on sand.
The rain fell, the floods came,
    and the winds blew and buffeted the house.
And it collapsed and was completely ruined."

When Jesus finished these words,
    the crowds were astonished at his teaching,
    for he taught them as one having authority,
    and not as their scribes.
The Gospel of the Lord.

or

Short Form: Matthew 7:21, 24–25
A wise man built his house on rock.

A reading from the holy Gospel according to Matthew
Jesus said to his disciples:

"Not everyone who says to me, 'Lord, Lord,'
   will enter the Kingdom of heaven,
   but only the one who does the will of my Father in heaven.

"Everyone who listens to these words of mine and acts on them
   will be like a wise man who built his house on rock.
The rain fell, the floods came,
   and the winds blew and buffeted the house.
But it did not collapse;
   it had been set solidly on rock."
The Gospel of the Lord.

F-4* / 805-4**
Matthew 19:3–6
What God has united, man must not separate.

A reading from the holy Gospel according to Matthew
Some Pharisees approached Jesus, and tested him, saying
   "Is it lawful for a man to divorce his wife for any cause whatever?"
He said in reply, "Have you not read that from the beginning
   the Creator made them male and female and said,
   For this reason a man shall leave his father and mother
   and be joined to his wife, and the two shall become one flesh?
So they are no longer two, but one flesh.
Therefore, what God has joined together, man must not separate."
The Gospel of the Lord.

F-5* / 805-5**
Matthew 22:35–40
This is the greatest and the first commandment. The second is like it.

A reading from the holy Gospel according to Matthew
One of the Pharisees, a scholar of the law, tested Jesus by asking,
   "Teacher, which commandment in the law is the greatest?"
He said to him,
   "You shall love the Lord, your God,
   with all your heart,
   with all your soul,
   and with all your mind.
This is the greatest and the first commandment.
The second is like it:

You shall love your neighbor as yourself.
The whole law and the prophets depend on these two commandments."
The Gospel of the Lord.

F-6* / 805-6**
Mark 10:6–9
They are no longer two, but one flesh.

A reading from the holy Gospel according to Mark
Jesus said:
"From the beginning of creation
God made them male and female.
For this reason a man shall leave his father and mother
and be joined to his wife,
and the two shall become one flesh.
So they are no longer two but one flesh.
Therefore what God has joined together,
no human being must separate.
The Gospel of the Lord.

F-7* / 805-7**
John 2:1–11
Jesus did this as the beginning of his signs in Cana in Galilee.

A reading from the holy Gospel according to John
There was a wedding in Cana in Galilee,
and the mother of Jesus was there.
Jesus and his disciples were also invited to the wedding.
When the wine ran short,
the mother of Jesus said to him,
"They have no wine."
And Jesus said to her,
"Woman, how does your concern affect me?
My hour has not yet come."
His mother said to the servers,
"Do whatever he tells you."
Now there were six stone water jars there for Jewish ceremonial washings,
each holding twenty to thirty gallons.
Jesus told them,
"Fill the jars with water."

So they filled them to the brim .
Then he told them,
    "Draw some out now and take it to the headwaiter."
So they took it.
And when the headwaiter tasted the water that had become wine,
        without knowing where it had come from
        (although the servants who had drawn the water knew),
        the headwaiter called the bridegroom and said to him,
        "Everyone serves good wine first,
        and then when people have drunk freely, an inferior one;
        but you have kept the good wine until now."
Jesus did this as the beginning of his signs in Cana in Galilee
        and so revealed his glory,
        and his disciples began to believe in him.
    The Gospel of the Lord.

F-8* / 805-8**
John 15: 9–12
Remain in my love.

A reading from the holy Gospel according to John
Jesus said to his disciples:
"As the Father loves me, so I also love you.
 Remain in my love.
 If you keep my commandments, you will remain in my love,
        just as I have kept my Father's commandments
        and remain in his love.

"I have told you this so that my joy might be in you
        and your joy might be complete.
 This is my commandment: love one another as I love you."
 The Gospel of the Lord.

F-9* 805-9**
John 15: 12–16
This is my commandment: love one another.

A reading from the holy Gospel according to John
Jesus said to his disciples;
"This is my commandment: love one another as I love you.
 No one has greater love than this,

to lay down one's life for one's friends.
You are my friends if you do what I command you.
I no longer call you slaves,
 because a slave does not know what his master is doing.
I have called you friends,
 because I have told you everything I have heard from my Father.
It was not you who chose me, but I who chose you
 and appointed you to go and bear fruit that will remain,
 so that whatever you ask the Father in my name he may give you."
The Gospel of the Lord.

F-10* / 805-10**
Long form: John 17:20–26
That they may be brought to perfection as one.

A reading from the holy Gospel according to John
Jesus raised his eyes to heaven and said:
"I pray not only for my disciples,
 but also for those who will believe in me through their word,
 so that they may all be one,
 as you, Father, are in me and I in you,
 that they also may be in us,
 that the world may believe that you sent me.
And I have given them the glory you gave me,
 so that they may be one, as we are one,
 I in them and you in me,
 that they may be brought to perfection as one,
 that the world may know that you sent me,
 and that you loved them even as you loved me.
Father, they are your gift to me.
I wish that where I am they also may be with me,
 that they may see my glory that you gave me,
 because you loved me before the foundation of the world.
Righteous Father, the world also does not know you,
 but I know you, and they know that you sent me.
 I made known to them your name and I will make it known,
 that the love with which you loved me
 may be in them and I in them."
The Gospel of the Lord.

or

Short Form: John 17: 20–23
That they may be brought to perfection as one.

A reading form the holy Gospel according to John
Jesus raised his eyes to heaven and said:
"Holy Father, I pray not only for these,
    but also for those who believe in me through their word,
    so that they may all be one,
    as you, Father, are in me and I in you,
    that they also may be in us,
    that the world may believe that you sent me.
And I have given them the glory you gave me,
    so that they may be one, as we are one,
    I in them and you in me,
    that they may be brought to perfection as one,
    that the world may know that you sent me,
    and that you loved them even as you loved me."
The Gospel of the Lord.

Homily

The Celebration of Matrimony *(During Mass)*

All stand, including the bride and bridegroom, and the priest addresses them in these or similar words:
Dearly beloved,
you have come together into the house of the Church,
so that in the presence of the Church's minister and the community
your intention to enter into Marriage
may be strengthened by the Lord with a sacred seal.
Christ abundantly blesses the love that binds you.
Through a special Sacrament,
he enriches and strengthens
those he has already consecrated by Holy Baptism,
that they may be faithful to each other for ever
and assume all the responsibilities of married life.
And so, in the presence of the Church,
I ask you to state your intentions.

Questions before the Consent

The priest then questions them about their freedom of choice, fidelity to each other, and the acceptance and upbringing of children, and each responds separately.
> N. and N. have you come here to enter into Marriage
> Without coercion,
> Freely and wholeheartedly?

The bridegroom and bride each say:
> **I have.**

The priest continues:
> Are you prepared, as you follow the path of Marriage,
> To love and honor each other
> For as long as you both shall live?
> *The bridegroom and bride each say:*
> **I am.**

The following question may be omitted, if circumstances suggest this, for example, if the couple are advanced in years.
> Are you prepared to accept children lovingly from God
> and to bring them up
> according to the law of Christ and his Church?

The bridegroom and bride each say:
> **I am.**

The Consent

The priest invites the couple to declare their consent:
> Since it is your intention to enter the covenant of Holy Matrimony,
> join your right hands and declare your consent
> before God and his Church.

They join their right hands.
The bridegroom says:
> I, N., take you, N., to be my wife.
> I promise to be faithful to you,
> in good times and in bad,

142

in sickness and in health,
to love you and to honor you
all the days of my life.

The bride says:
I, N., take you, N., to be my husband.
I promise to be faithful to you,
in good times and in bad,
in sickness and in health,
to love you and to honor you
all the days of my life.

The following alternative form may be used:
The bridegroom says:
I, N., take you, N., for my lawful wife,
to have and to hold, from this day forward,
for better, for worse,
for richer, for poorer,
in sickness and in health,
to love and to cherish
until death do us part.

The bride says:
I, N., take you, N., for my lawful husband,
to have and to hold, from this day forward,
for better, for worse,
for richer, for poorer,
in sickness and in health,
to love and to cherish
until death do us part.

If, however, it seems preferable for pastoral reasons, the priest may obtain the consent of the contracting parties through questioning. First, he asks the bridegroom:
N., do you take N. to be your wife?
Do you promise to be faithful to her
in good times and in bad,
in sickness and in health,
to love her and to honor her
all the days of your life?

The bridegroom replies:
I do.

Next, the Priest asks the bride:
N., do you take N. to be your husband?
Do you promise to be faithful to him
in good times and in bad,
in sickness and in health,
to love him and to honor him
all the days of your life?

The bride replies:
I do.

The following alternative form may be used:
First, he asks the bridegroom:
N., do you take N. for your lawful wife,
To have and to hold, from this day forward,
for better, for worse,
for richer, for poorer,
in sickness and in health,
to love and to cherish
until death do you part?

The bridegroom replies:
I do.

Next, the Priest asks the bride:
N., do you take N. for your lawful husband,
To have and to hold, from this day forward,
for better, for worse,
for richer, for poorer,
in sickness and in health,
to love and to cherish
until death do you part?

The bride replies:
I do.

The Reception of the Consent

Receiving their consent, the Priest says to the bride and bridegroom:
May the Lord in his kindness strengthen the consent
you have declared before the Church,
and graciously bring to fulfillment his blessings within you.
what God joins together, let no one put asunder.
***R.* Amen.**

or

May the God of Abraham, the God of Isaac, the God of Jacob,
the God who joined together our first parents in paradise,
strengthen and bless in Christ
the consent you have declared before the Church,
so that what God joins together, no one may put asunder.
***R.* Amen.**

The Blessing and Giving of Rings

Priest:

I-1*

May the Lord bless ✠ these rings,
which you will give to each other
as the sign of love and fidelity.
***R.* Amen.**

I-2*

Bless, O Lord, these rings,
which we bless ✠ in your name,
so that those who wear them
may remain faithful to each other,
abide in peace and in your will,
and live always in mutual charity.
Through Christ our Lord.
***R.* Amen.**

I-3*

Bless ✠ and sanctify your servants
in their love, O Lord,

And let these rings, a sign of their faithfulness,
remind them of their love for one another.
Through Christ our Lord.
R. **Amen.**

The husband places his wife's ring on her ring finger, saying, as the circum-
stances so suggest:
N., receive this ring
as a sign of my love and fidelity.
In the name of the Father, and of the Son,
and of the Holy Spirit.

Likewise, the wife places her husband's ring on his finger, saying, as the cir-
cumstances so suggest:
N., receive this ring
as a sign of my love and fidelity.
In the name of the Father, and of the Son,
and of the Holy Spirit.

The Blessing and Giving of the *Arras*

If the occasion so suggests, the rite of blessing and giving of the arras (coins)
may take place following the blessing and giving of rings.

The Priest says:
Bless, ✠ O Lord, these *arras*
that N. and N. will give to each other
and pour over them the abundance of your good gifts.

The husband takes the arras and hands them over to his wife, saying:
N., receive these *arras* as a pledge of God's blessing
and a sign of the good gifts we will share.

The wife takes the arras and hands them over to the husband, saying:
N., receive these *arras* as a pledge of God's blessing
and a sign of the good gifts we will share.

The Universal Prayer

The Universal Prayer (prayer of the faithful) follows; these are provided
as a sample.

Dear brothers and sisters,
as we call to mind the special gift of grace and charity
by which God has been pleased to crown and consecrate
the love of our sister N. and our brother N.,
let us commend them to the Lord.

That these faithful Christians, N. and N.,
newly joined in Holy Matrimony,
may always enjoy health and well-being,
let us pray to the Lord.
R. **Lord, we ask you, hear our prayer.**

Or another appropriate response of the people.

That he will bless their covenant
as he chose to sanctify marriage at Cana in Galilee,
let us pray to the Lord. *R.*

That they be granted perfect and fruitful love,
peace and strength,
and that they bear faithful witness to the name of Christian,
let us pray to the Lord. *R.*

That the Christian people
may grow in virtue day by day
and that all who are burdened by any need
may receive the help of grace from above,
let us pray to the Lord. *R.*

That the grace of the Sacrament
will be renewed by the Holy Spirit
in all married persons here present,
let us pray to the Lord. *R.*

Graciously pour out upon this husband and wife, O Lord,
the Spirit of your love,
to make them one heart and one soul,
so that nothing whatever may divide those you have joined
and no harm come to those you have filled with your blessing.
Through Christ our Lord.
R. **Amen.**

or

Dear brothers and sisters,
let us accompany this new family with our prayers,
that the mutual love of this couple may grow daily
and that God in his kindness
will sustain all families throughout the world.

For this bride and groom,
and for their well-being as a family,
let us pray to the Lord.
R. **Lord, we ask you, hear our prayer.**

Or another appropriate response of the people.

For their relatives and friends,
and for all who have assisted this couple,
let us pray to the Lord. *R.*

For young people preparing to enter Marriage,
and for all whom the Lord is calling to another state in life,
let us pray to the Lord. *R.*

For all families throughout the world
and for lasting peace among all people,
let us pray to the Lord. *R.*

For all members of our families
who have passed from this world,
and for all the departed,
let us pray to the Lord. *R.*

For the Church, the holy People of God,
and for unity among all Christians,
let us pray to the Lord. *R.*

Lord Jesus, who are present in our midst,
as N. and N. seal their union
accept our prayer
and fill us with your Spirit.
Who live and reign for ever and ever.
R. **Amen.**

148

Liturgy of the Eucharist

Prayer Over the Offerings

With hands extended, the priest sings or says one of the following:

K-1*
> Receive, we pray, O Lord,
> the offering made on the occasion
> of this sealing of the sacred bond of Marriage,
> and, just as your goodness is its origin,
> may your providence guide its course.
> Through Christ our Lord.
> *R.* **Amen.**

K-2*
> Receive in your kindness, Lord,
> The offerings we bring in gladness before you,
> And in your fatherly love
> Watch over those you have joined in a sacramental covenant.
> Though Christ our Lord.
> *R.* **Amen.**

K-3*
> Show favor to our supplications, O Lord,
> And receive with a kindly countenance
> The oblations we offer for these your servants,
> Joined now in a holy covenant,
> That through these mysteries
> They may be strengthened
> In love for one another and for you.
> Through Christ our Lord.
> *R.* **Amen.**

Preface

The priest begins the eucharistic prayer. With hands extended, he sings or says:

L-1*
The dignity of the Marriage covenant.
> It is truly right and just, our duty and our salvation,

always and everywhere to give you thanks,
Lord, holy Father, almighty and eternal God.

For you have forged the covenant of Marriage
as a sweet yoke of harmony
and an unbreakable bond of peace,
so that the chaste and fruitful love of holy Matrimony
may serve to increase the children you adopt as your own.

By your providence and grace, O Lord,
you accomplish the wonder of this twofold design:
that, while the birth of children brings beauty to the world,
their rebirth in Baptism gives increase to the Church,
through Christ our Lord.

Through him, with the Angels and all the Saints,
we sing the hymn of your praise,
as without end we acclaim:

L-2*

The great Sacrament of Matrimony.

It is truly right and just, our duty and our salvation,
always and everywhere to give you thanks,
Lord, holy Father, almighty and eternal God,
through Christ our Lord.

For in him you have made a new covenant with your people,
so that, as you have redeemed man and woman
by the mystery of Christ's Death and Resurrection,
so in Christ you might make them partakers of divine nature
and joint heirs with him of heavenly glory.

In the union of husband and wife
you give a sign of Christ's loving gift of grace,
so that the Sacrament we celebrate
might draw us back more deeply
into the wondrous design of your love.

And so, with the Angels and all the Saints,
we praise you, and without end we acclaim:

L-3*

Matrimony as a sign of divine love.

It is truly right and just, our duty and our salvation,
always and everywhere to give you thanks,
Lord, holy Father, almighty and eternal God.

For you willed that the human race,
created by the gift of your goodness,
should be raised to such high dignity
that in the union of husband and wife
you might bestow a true image of your love.

For those you created out of charity
you call to the law of charity without ceasing
and grant them a share in your eternal charity.

And so, the Sacrament of holy Matrimony,
as the abiding sign of your own love,
consecrates the love of man and woman,
through Christ our Lord.
Through him, with the Angels and all the Saints,
we sing the hymn of your praise,
as without end we acclaim:

Commemoration of the Couple in the Eucharistic Prayer

Eucharistic Prayer I

*The proper form of the Hanc igitur (*Therefore, Lord, we pray*) is said. The words in parentheses may be omitted, if the occasion so suggests.*

Therefore, Lord, we pray:
graciously accept this oblation of our service,
the offering of your servants N. and N.
and of your whole family,
who entreat your majesty on their behalf;
and as you have brought them to their wedding day,
so (gladden them with your gift of the children they desire and)
bring them in your kindness
to the length of days for which they hope.
(Through Christ our Lord. Amen.)

Eucharistic Prayer II

After the words and all the clergy, *the following is added:*
    Be mindful also, Lord, of N. and N.,
    whom you have brought to their wedding day,
    so that by your grace
    they may abide in mutual love and in peace.

Eucharistic Prayer III

After the words whom you have summoned before you, *the following is added:*
    Strengthen, we pray, in the grace of Marriage N. and N.,
    whom you have brought happily to their wedding day,
    that under your protection
    they may always be faithful in their lives
    to the covenant they have sealed in your presence.
    In your compassion, O merciful Father,
    gather to yourself all your children
    scattered throughout the world.

The Blessing and Placing of the *Lazo* or the Veil

According to local customs, the rite of blessing and imposition of the lazo *(wedding garland) or of the veil may take place before the Nuptial Blessing. The spouses remain kneeling in their place. If the* lazo *has not been placed earlier, and it is now convenient to do so, it may be placed at this time, or else, a veil is placed over the head of the wife and the shoulders of the husband, thus symbolizing the bond that unites them.*

The Priest says:
    Bless, ✠ O Lord, this *lazo* (or: this veil),
    a symbol of the indissoluble union
    that N. and N. have established from this day forward
    before you and with your help.

The lazo *(or the veil) is held by two family members or friends and is placed over the shoulders of the newly married couple.*

The Lord's Prayer
The Nuptial Blessing

After the Lord's Prayer, the prayer Deliver us *is omitted. The priest faces the bride and bridegroom and, with hands joined, says:*

M-1*

    Dear brothers and sisters,
    let us humbly pray to the Lord
    that on these his servants, now married in Christ,
    he may mercifully pour out
    the blessing of his grace
    and make of one heart in love
    (by the Sacrament of Christ's Body and Blood)
    those he has joined by a holy covenant.

All pray in silence for a while. Then the Priest, with hands extended over the bride and bridegroom continues:

    O God, who by your mighty power
    created all things out of nothing,
    and, when you had set in place
    the beginnings of the universe,
    formed man and woman in your own image,
    making the woman an inseparable helpmate to the man,
    that they might no longer be two, but one flesh,
    and taught that what you were pleased to make one
    must never be divided;

    O God, who consecrated the bond of Marriage
    by so great a mystery
    that in the wedding covenant you foreshadowed
    the Sacrament of Christ and his Church;

    O God, by whom woman is joined to man
    and the companionship they had in the beginning
    is endowed with the one blessing
    not forfeited by original sin
    nor washed away by the flood.

    Look now with favor on these your servants,
    joined together in Marriage,
    who ask to be strengthened by your blessing.

Send down on them the grace of the Holy Spirit
and pour your love into their hearts,
that they may remain faithful in the Marriage covenant.

May the grace of love and peace
abide in your daughter N.,
and let her always follow the example of those holy women
whose praises are sung in the Scriptures.

May her husband entrust his heart to her,
so that, acknowledging her as his equal
and his joint heir to the life of grace,
he may show her due honor
and cherish her always
with the love that Christ has for his Church.

And now, Lord, we implore you:
may these your servants
hold fast to the faith and keep your commandments;
made one in the flesh,
may they be blameless in all they do;
and with the strength that comes from the Gospel,
may they bear true witness to Christ before all;
(may they be blessed with children,
and prove themselves virtuous parents,
who live to see their children's children).

And grant that,
reaching at last together the fullness of years
for which they hope,
they may come to the life of the blessed
in the Kingdom of Heaven.
Through Christ our Lord.
R. Amen.

*If one or both of the parties will not be receiving communion, the words in
the introduction to the nuptial blessing,* through the sacrament of the body
and blood of Christ, *may be omitted.*

*In the last paragraph of this prayer, the words in parentheses may be
omitted whenever circumstances suggest it, if, for example, the couple is
advanced in years.*

M-2*

Let us pray to the Lord for this bride and groom,
who come to the altar as they begin their married life,
that (partaking of the Body and Blood of Christ)
they may always be bound together by love for one another.

All pray in silence for a while. Then the Priest, with hands extended over the bride and bridegroom continues:

Holy Father,
who formed man in your own image,
male and female you created them,
so that as husband and wife, united in body and heart,
they might fulfill their calling in the world;
O God, who, to reveal the great design you formed in your love,
willed that the love of spouses for each other
should foreshadow the covenant you graciously made with your people,
so that, by fulfillment of the sacramental sign,
the mystical marriage of Christ with his Church
might become manifest
in the union of husband and wife among your faithful;
Graciously stretch out your right hand
over these your servants (N. and N.), we pray,
and pour into their hearts the power of the Holy Spirit.

Grant, O Lord,
that, as they enter upon this sacramental union,
they may share with one another the gifts of your love
and, by being for each other a sign of your presence,
become one heart and one mind.

May they also sustain, O Lord, by their deeds
the home they are forming
(and prepare their children
to become members of your heavenly household
by raising them in the way of the Gospel).

Graciously crown with your blessings your daughter N.,
so that, by being a good wife (and mother),
she may bring warmth to her home with a love that is pure
and adorn it with welcoming graciousness.

Bestow a heavenly blessing also, O Lord,
on N., your servant,
that he may be a worthy, good and
faithful husband (and a provident father).

Grant, holy Father,
that, desiring to approach your table
as a couple joined in Marriage in your presence,
they may one day have the joy
of taking part in your great banquet in heaven.
Through Christ our Lord.
R. **Amen.**

M-3*

Let us humbly invoke by our prayers, dear brothers and sisters,
God's blessing upon this bride and groom,
that in his kindness he may favor with his help
those on whom he has bestowed the Sacrament of Matrimony.

*All pray in silence for a while. Then the Priest, with hands extended over the
bride and bridegroom continues:*
Holy Father, maker of the whole world,
who created man and woman in your own image
and willed that their union be crowned with your blessing,
we humbly beseech you for these your servants,
who are joined today in the Sacrament of Matrimony.

May your abundant blessing, Lord,
come down upon this bride, N.,
and upon N., her companion for life,
and may the power of your Holy Spirit
set their hearts aflame from on high,
so that, living out together the gift of Matrimony,
they may (adorn their family with children
and) enrich the Church.

In happiness may they praise you, O Lord,
in sorrow may they seek you out;
may they have the joy of your presence

to assist them in their toil,
and know that you are near
to comfort them in their need;
let them pray to you in the holy assembly
and bear witness to you in the world,
and after a happy old age,
together with the circle of friends that surrounds them,
may they come to the Kingdom of Heaven.
Through Christ our Lord.
R. **Amen.**

The Sign of Peace
Communion
Prayer After Communion

N-1*

By the power of this sacrifice, O Lord,
accompany with your loving favor
what in your providence you have instituted,
so as to make of one heart in love
those you have already joined in this holy union
(and replenished with the one Bread and the one Chalice).
Through Christ our Lord.

N-2*

Having been made partakers at your table,
we pray, O Lord,
that those who are united by the Sacrament of Marriage
may always hold fast to you
and proclaim your name to the world.
Through Christ our Lord.

N-3*

Grant, we pray, almighty God,
that the power of the Sacrament we have received
may find growth in these your servants
and that the effects of the sacrifice we have offered
may be felt by us all.
Through Christ our Lord.

Concluding Rite

Solemn or Final Blessing

At the end of Mass, the Priest, with hands extended over the bride and bridegroom, says:

O-1*

May God the eternal Father
keep you of one heart in love for one another,
that the peace of Christ may dwell in you
and abide always in your home.
R. **Amen.**

May you be blessed in your children,
have solace in your friends
and enjoy true peace with everyone.
R. **Amen.**
May you be witnesses in the world to God's charity,
so that the afflicted and needy who have known your kindness
may one day receive you thankfully
into the eternal dwelling of God.
R. **Amen.**

And he blesses all present, adding:

And may almighty God bless all of you, who are gathered here,
the Father, and the Son, ✠ and the Holy Spirit.
R. **Amen.**

O-2*

May God the all-powerful Father grant you his joy
and bless you in your children.
R. **Amen.**
May the Only Begotten Son of God
stand by you with compassion in good times and in bad.
R. **Amen.**
May the Holy Spirit of God
always pour forth his love into your hearts.
R. **Amen.**

And he blesses all present, adding:
    And may almighty God bless all of you, who are gathered here,
the Father, and the Son, ✠ and the Holy Spirit.
***R.* Amen.**

O-3*
    May the Lord Jesus,
who graced the marriage at Cana by his presence,
bless you and your loved ones.
***R.* Amen.**
May he, who loved the Church to the end,
unceasingly pour his love into your hearts.
***R.* Amen.**

May the Lord grant
that, bearing witness to faith in his Resurrection,
you may await with joy the blessed hope to come.
***R.* Amen.**

And he blesses all present, adding:
    And may almighty God bless all of you, who are gathered here,
the Father, and the Son, ✠ and the Holy Spirit.
***R.* Amen.**

Dismissal

THE ORDER OF CELEBRATING MATRIMONY WITHOUT MASS

Introductory Rites

After the procession, welcome and the Sign of the Cross has been made, the minister greets those present, saying:
> Grace to you and peace from God our Father
> and the Lord Jesus Christ.

Or some other suitable greeting, taken from The Roman Missal. All reply:
> **And with your spirit.**

Then the minister extends his hands and sings or says the opening prayer, at the end of which the people respond:
> **Amen.**

> We have come rejoicing into the house of the Lord
> for this celebration, dear brothers and sisters,
> and now we stand with N. and N.
> on the day they intend to form a home of their own.
> For them this is a moment of unique importance.
> So let us support them
> with our affection,
> with our friendship,
> and with our prayer as their brothers and sisters.
> Let us listen attentively with them
> to the word that God speaks to us today.
> Then, with holy Church,
> let us humbly pray to God the Father,
> through Christ our Lord,
> for this couple, his servants,
> that he lovingly accept them,
> bless them,
> and make them always one.
> *R.* **Amen.**

or

> N. and N., the Church shares your joy
> and warmly welcomes you,

together with your families and friends,
as today,
in the presence of God our Father,
you establish between yourselves
a lifelong partnership.
May the Lord hear you on this your joyful day.
May he send you help from heaven and protect you.
May he grant you your hearts' desire
and fulfill every one of your prayers.
R. **Amen.**

Then, with hands extended, he says this prayer:

Be attentive to our prayers, O Lord,
and in your kindness
pour out your grace on these your servants (N. and N.),
that, coming together before your altar,
they may be confirmed in love for one another.
Through Christ our Lord.
R. **Amen.**

or

O God, who consecrated the bond of Marriage
by so great a mystery
that in the wedding covenant you foreshadow
the Sacrament of Christ and his Church,
grant, we pray, to these your servants,
that what they receive in faith
they may live out in deeds.
Through our Lord Jesus Christ, your Son,
who lives and reigns with you in the unity of the Holy Spirit,
one God, for ever and ever.
R. **Amen.**

or

O God, who in creating the human race
willed that man and wife should be one,

join, we pray, in a bond of inseparable love
these your servants who are to be united in the covenant of Marriage,
so that, as you make their love fruitful,
they may become, by your grace, witnesses to charity itself.
Through our Lord Jesus Christ, your Son,
who lives and reigns with you in the unity of the Holy Spirit,
one God, for ever and ever.
R. **Amen.**

or

Be attentive to our prayers, O Lord,
and in your kindness
pour out your grace on these your servants (N. and N.),
that, coming together before your altar,
they may be confirmed in love for one another.
Through our Lord Jesus Christ, your Son,
who lives and reigns with you in the unity of the Holy Spirit,
one God, for ever and ever.
R. **Amen.**

or

Grant, we pray, almighty God,
that these your servants,
now to be joined by the Sacrament of Matrimony,
may grow in the faith they profess
and enrich your Church with faithful offspring.
Through our Lord Jesus Christ, your Son,
who lives and reigns with you in the unity of the Holy Spirit,
one God, for ever and ever.
R. **Amen.**

or

Be attentive to our prayers, O Lord,
and in your kindness uphold
what you have established for the increase of the human race,
so that the union you have created
may be kept safe by your assistance.

Through our Lord Jesus Christ, your Son,
who lives and reigns with you in the unity of the Holy Spirit,
one God, for ever and ever.
R. **Amen.**

or

O God, who since the beginning of the world
have blessed the increase of offspring,
show favor to our supplications
and pour forth the help of your blessing
on these your servants (N. and N.),
so that in the union of Marriage
they may be bound together
in mutual affection,
in likeness of mind,
and in shared holiness.
Through our Lord Jesus Christ, your Son,
who lives and reigns with you in the unity of the Holy Spirit,
one God, for ever and ever.
R. **Amen.**

Liturgy of the Word

See Readings on pages 109–140 in "The Order or Celebrating Matrimony Within Mass."

The Celebration of Matrimony

With all standing, including the couple and the witnesses, who are positioned near them, the minister addresses the couple in these or similar words:
Dearly beloved,
you have come together into the house of the Church,
so that in the presence of the Church's minister and the community
your intention to enter into Marriage
may be strengthened by the Lord with a sacred seal.
Christ abundantly blesses the love that binds you.
Through a special Sacrament,
he enriches and strengthens

those he has already consecrated by Holy Baptism,
that they may be faithful to each other for ever
and assume all the responsibilities of married life.
And so, in the presence of the Church,
I ask you to state your intentions.

Questions before the Consent

The minister then questions them about their freedom of choice, fidelity to each other, and the acceptance and upbringing of children, and each responds separately.
N. and N. have you come here to enter into Marriage
Without coercion,
Freely and wholeheartedly?

The bridegroom and bride each say:
I have.

The minister continues:
Are you prepared, as you follow the path of Marriage,
To love and honor each other
For as long as you both shall live?

The bridegroom and bride each say:
I am.

The following question may be omitted, if circumstances suggest this, for example, if the couple are advanced in years.
Are you prepared to accept children lovingly from God
and to bring them up
according to the law of Christ and his Church?

The bridegroom and bride each say:
I am.

The Consent

The minister invites the couple to declare their consent:
Since it is your intention to enter the covenant of Holy Matrimony,
join your right hands and declare your consent
before God and his Church.

They join their right hands.
The bridegroom says:
    I, N., take you, N., to be my wife.
    I promise to be faithful to you,
    in good times and in bad,
    in sickness and in health,
    to love you and to honor you
    all the days of my life.

The bride says:
    I, N., take you, N., to be my husband.
    I promise to be faithful to you,
    in good times and in bad,
    in sickness and in health,
    to love you and to honor you
    all the days of my life.

The following alternative form may be used:
The bridegroom says:
    I, N., take you, N., for my lawful wife,
    to have and to hold, from this day forward,
    for better, for worse,
    for richer, for poorer,
    in sickness and in health,
    to love and to cherish
    until death do us part.

The bride says:
    I, N., take you, N., for my lawful husband,
    to have and to hold, from this day forward,
    for better, for worse,
    for richer, for poorer,
    in sickness and in health,
    to love and to cherish
    until death do us part.

If, however, it seems preferable for pastoral reasons, the priest may obtain the consent of the contracting parties through questioning.
First, he asks the bridegroom:
    N., do you take N. to be your wife?
    Do you promise to be faithful to her

in good times and in bad,
in sickness and in health,
to love her and to honor her
all the days of your life?

The bridegroom replies:
I do.

Next, the Minister asks the bride:
N., do you take N. to be your husband?
Do you promise to be faithful to him
in good times and in bad,
in sickness and in health,
to love him and to honor him
all the days of your life?

The bride replies:
I do.

The following alternative form may be used:
First, he asks the bridegroom:
N., do you take N. for your lawful wife,
To have and to hold, from this day forward,
for better, for worse,
for richer, for poorer,
in sickness and in health,
to love and to cherish
until death do you part?

The bridegroom replies:
I do.

Next, the Minister asks the bride:
N., do you take N. for your lawful husband,
To have and to hold, from this day forward,
for better, for worse,
for richer, for poorer,
in sickness and in health,
to love and to cherish
until death do you part?

The bride replies:
I do.

The Reception of the Consent

Receiving their consent, the Minister says to the bride and bridegroom:
May the Lord in his kindness, strengthen the consent
you have declared before the Church,
and graciously bring to fulfillment his blessings within you.
What God joins together, let no one put asunder.
R. **Amen.**

or

May the God of Abraham, the God of Isaac, the God of Jacob,
the God who joined together our first parents in paradise,
strengthen and bless in Christ
the consent you have declared before the Church,
so that what God joins together, no one may put asunder.
R. **Amen.**

The Blessing and Giving of Rings

Minister:

I-1*
May the Lord bless ✠ these rings,
which you will give to each other
as the sign of love and fidelity.
R. **Amen.**

I-2*
Bless, O Lord, these rings,
which we bless ✠ in your name,
so that those who wear them
may remain faithful to each other,
abide in peace and in your will,
and live always in mutual charity.
Through Christ our Lord.
R. **Amen.**

I-3*

> Bless ✠ and sanctify your servants
> in their love, O Lord,
> And let these rings, a sign of their faithfulness,
> remind them of their love for one another.
> Through Christ our Lord.
> **R. Amen.**

The husband places his wife's ring on her ring finger, saying, as the circumstances so suggest:

> N., receive this ring
> as a sign of my love and fidelity.
> In the name of the Father, and of the Son,
> and of the Holy Spirit.

Likewise, the wife places her husband's ring on his finger, saying, as the circumstances so suggest:

> N., receive this ring
> as a sign of my love and fidelity.
> In the name of the Father, and of the Son,
> and of the Holy Spirit.

The Blessing and Giving of the *Arras*

If the occasion so suggests, the rite of blessing and giving of the arras *(coins) may take place following the blessing and giving of rings.*

The minister says:

> Bless, ✠ O Lord, these *arras*
> that N. and N. will give to each other
> and pour over them the abundance of your good gifts.

The husband takes the arras and hands them over to his wife, saying:

> N., receive these *arras* as a pledge of God's blessing
> and a sign of the good gifts we will share.

The wife takes the arras and hands them over to the husband, saying:

> N., receive these *arras* as a pledge of God's blessing
> and a sign of the good gifts we will share.

The Universal Prayer

See Universal Prayers on pages 145–147 in "The Order of Celebrating Matrimony Within Mass."

If the rubrics call for it, the profession of faith is said after the general intercessions.

The Blessing and Placing of the *Lazo* or the Veil

According to local customs, the rite of blessing and imposition of the lazo *(wedding garland) or of the veil may take place before the Nuptial Blessing. The spouses remain at their place and kneel. Then, if it is convenient to do so, the* lazo *may be placed at this time, or else, a veil is placed over the head of the wife and the shoulders of the husband, thus symbolizing the bond that unites them.*

The one who presides says:
  Bless, ✠ O Lord, this *lazo* (or: this veil),
  a symbol of the indissoluble union
  that N. and N. have established from this day forward
  before you and with your help.

The lazo *(or the veil) is held by two family members or friends and is placed over the shoulders of the newly married couple.*

Nuptial Blessings

See Nuptial Blessings on pages 152–156 in "The Order of Celebrating Matrimony Within Mass."

Conclusion of the Celebration

The Lord's Prayer
Blessing
See Concluding Rites on pages 157–158 in "The Order of Celebrating Matrimony Within Mass."

THE ORDER OF CELEBRATING MATRIMONY BETWEEN A CATHOLIC AND A CATECHUMEN OR A NON-CHRISTIAN

The Rite of Reception

At the appointed time, the one who presides, the Priest or Deacon, wearing an alb and stole, and even a cope (or a dalmatic, for a Deacon) of the color white or a festive color, goes with the servers to the door of the church or to the place that has been chosen, where he receives the bridal party and warmly greets them.

After this, the one who presides, the servers, the couple, the witnesses, and all present go to the seats prepared for each one.

Then, in these or similar words, the one who presides addresses them to dispose them inwardly for the celebration of Marriage:
N. and N., the Church shares your joy
and warmly welcomes you,
together with your families and friends,
as today,
in the presence of God our Father,
you establish between yourselves
a lifelong partnership.
May the Lord hear you on this your joyful day.
May he send you help from heaven and protect you.
May he grant you your hearts' desire
and fulfill every one of your prayers.
R. **Amen.**

If, however, circumstances so suggest, the Rite of Reception is omitted and the celebration of Marriage begins with the Liturgy of the Word.

Liturgy of the Word

The Liturgy of the Word follows in the usual manner with texts found on pages 109–140 in "The Order of Celebrating Matrimony Within Mass." There may be one or two readings. If, however, circumstances make this more desirable, there may be only one reading. At least one reading that explicitly speaks of Marriage must always be chosen.

The Celebration of Matrimony

With all standing, including the couple and the witnesses, who are positioned near them, the one who presides addresses the couple in these or similar words:

Dearly beloved,
you have come together here
before a minister of the Church
and in the presence of the community
so that your intention to enter into Marriage
may be strengthened by the Lord with a sacred seal,
and your love may be enriched with his blessing,
so that you may have strength
to be faithful to each other for ever
and to assume all the responsibilities of married life.
And so, in the presence of the Church,
I ask you to state your intentions.

Questions before the Consent

The one who presides then questions them about their freedom of choice, fidelity to each other, and the acceptance and upbringing of children, and each responds separately.

N. and N. have you come here to enter into Marriage
Without coercion,
Freely and wholeheartedly?

The bridegroom and bride each say:
I have.

The minister continues:

Are you prepared, as you follow the path of Marriage,
To love and honor each other
For as long as you both shall live?

The bridegroom and bride each say:
I am.

The following question may be omitted, if circumstances suggest this, for example, if the couple are advanced in years.

Are you prepared to accept children lovingly from God
and to bring them up
according to the law of Christ and his Church?

The bridegroom and bride each say:
I am.

The Consent

The one who presides invites the couple to declare their consent:
Since it is your intention to enter the covenant of Holy Matrimony,
join your right hands and declare your consent
before God and his Church.

They join their right hands.
The bridegroom says:
I, N., take you, N., to be my wife.
I promise to be faithful to you,
in good times and in bad,
in sickness and in health,
to love you and to honor you
all the days of my life.

The bride says:
I, N., take you, N., to be my husband.
I promise to be faithful to you,
in good times and in bad,
in sickness and in health,
to love you and to honor you
all the days of my life.

The following alternative form may be used:
The bridegroom says:
I, N., take you, N., for my lawful wife,
to have and to hold, from this day forward,
for better, for worse,
for richer, for poorer,
in sickness and in health,
to love and to cherish
until death do us part.

The bride says:
> I, N., take you, N., for my lawful husband,
> to have and to hold, from this day forward,
> for better, for worse,
> for richer, for poorer,
> in sickness and in health,
> to love and to cherish
> until death do us part.

If, however, it seems preferable for pastoral reasons, the one who presides may obtain the consent of the contracting parties through questioning.
First, he asks the bridegroom:
> N., do you take N. to be your wife?
> Do you promise to be faithful to her
> in good times and in bad,
> in sickness and in health,
> to love her and to honor her
> all the days of your life?

The bridegroom replies:
> **I do.**

Next, the Minister asks the bride:
> N., do you take N. to be your husband?
> Do you promise to be faithful to him
> in good times and in bad,
> in sickness and in health,
> to love him and to honor him
> all the days of your life?

The bride replies:
> **I do.**

The following alternative form may be used:
First, he asks the bridegroom:
> N., do you take N. for your lawful wife,
> To have and to hold, from this day forward,
> for better, for worse,
> for richer, for poorer,
> in sickness and in health,
> to love and to cherish
> until death do you part?

The bridegroom replies:
I do.

Next, the Minister asks the bride:
N., do you take N. for your lawful husband,
To have and to hold, from this day forward,
for better, for worse,
for richer, for poorer,
in sickness and in health,
to love and to cherish
until death do you part?

The bride replies:
I do.

The Reception of the Consent

Receiving their consent, the one who presides says to the bride and bride-groom:
May the Lord in his kindness, strengthen the consent
you have declared before the Church,
and graciously bring to fulfillment his blessings within you.
what God joins together, let no one put asunder.
R. **Amen.**

or

May the God of Abraham, the God of Isaac, the God of Jacob,
the God who joined together our first parents in paradise,
strengthen and bless in Christ
the consent you have declared before the Church,
so that what God joins together, no one may put asunder.
R. **Amen.**

The Blessing and Giving of Rings

Priest or Deacon:

I-1*
May the Lord bless ✠ these rings,
which you will give to each other

as the sign of love and fidelity.
R. Amen.

I-2*

Bless, O Lord, these rings,
which we bless ✠ in your name,
so that those who wear them
may remain faithful to each other,
abide in peace and in your will,
and live always in mutual charity.
Through Christ our Lord.
R. Amen.

I-3*

Bless ✠ and sanctify your servants
in their love, O Lord,
And let these rings, a sign of their faithfulness,
remind them of their love for one another.
Through Christ our Lord.
R. Amen.

The husband places his wife's ring on her ring finger, saying, as the circumstances so suggest:
N., receive this ring
as a sign of my love and fidelity.
In the name of the Father, and of the Son,
and of the Holy Spirit.

Likewise, the wife places her husband's ring on his finger, saying, as the circumstances so suggest:
N., receive this ring
as a sign of my love and fidelity.
In the name of the Father, and of the Son,
and of the Holy Spirit.

The Blessing and Giving of the *Arras*

If the occasion so suggests, the rite of blessing and giving of the arras *(coins) may take place following the blessing and giving of rings.*

The one who presides says:
Bless, ✠ O Lord, these *arras*

that N. and N. will give to each other
and pour over them the abundance of your good gifts.

The husband takes the arras and hands them over to his wife, saying:
  N., receive these *arras* as a pledge of God's blessing
  and a sign of the good gifts we will share.

The wife takes the arras and hands them over to the husband, saying:
  N., receive these *arras* as a pledge of God's blessing
  and a sign of the good gifts we will share.

The Universal Prayer

*See the Universal Prayers on pages 145–147 in "The Order of Celebrating
Matrimony Within Mass."*
  *If the rubrics call for it, the profession of faith is said after the general
intercessions.*

The Our Father
The Blessing and Placing of the *Lazo* or the Veil

According to local customs, the rite of blessing and imposition of the lazo
*(wedding garland) or of the veil may take place before the Nuptial Blessing.
The spouses remain at their place and kneel. Then, if it is convenient to do
so, the* lazo *may be placed at this time, or else, a veil is placed over the head
of the wife and the shoulders of the husband, thus symbolizing the bond that
unites them.*

The one who presides says:
  Bless, ✠ O Lord, this *lazo* (or: this veil),
  a symbol of the indissoluble union
  that N. and N. have established from this day forward
  before you and with your help.

The lazo *(or the veil) is held by two family members or friends and is placed
over the shoulders of the newly married couple.*

The Nuptial Blessing

*As a rule, the Nuptial Blessing is said over the bride and bridegroom. The
bride and bridegroom kneel at their place, if circumstances suggest this.*

Then, the Priest (or Deacon) continues, with hands joined:
Now let us humbly invoke God's blessing
upon this bride and groom,
that in his kindness he may favor with his help
those on whom he has bestowed the bond of Marriage.

And all pray in silence for a while.

Then, the Priest (or Deacon), standing and turned toward the bride and bridegroom with hands extended over them, continues:
Holy Father, maker of the whole world,
who created man and woman in your own image
and willed that their union be crowned with your blessing,
we humbly beseech you for these your servants,
who are joined today in the Marriage covenant.
May your abundant blessing, Lord,
come down upon this bride, N.,
and upon N., her companion for life,
and may the power of your Holy Spirit
set their hearts aflame from on high,
so that, living out together the gift of Matrimony,
they may be known for the integrity of their conduct
(and be recognized as virtuous parents).
In happiness may they praise you, O Lord,
in sorrow may they seek you out;
may they have the joy of your presence
to assist them in their toil,
and know that you are near
to comfort them in their need;
and after a happy old age,
together with the circle of friends that surrounds them,
may they come to the Kingdom of Heaven.
Through Christ our Lord.
R. Amen.

If, because of circumstances, the Nuptial Blessing is omitted, this prayer is spoken over the bride and bridegroom:
Be attentive to our prayers, O Lord,
and in your kindness uphold
what you have established for the increase of the human race,
so that the union you have created

may be kept safe by your assistance.
Through Christ our Lord.
R. **Amen.**

The Conclusion of the Celebration

Then, the Priest (or Deacon) blesses the people, saying:
May almighty God bless all of you, who are gathered here,
the Father, and the Son, ✠ and the Holy Spirit.
R. **Amen.**

Notes

All references from the *Catechism of the Catholic Church* are specified by paragraph numbers.

Chapter One: Seeking Your Vision of Love

1. The term "pizza-love" comes from May Beth Bonacci's *Real Love* (San Francisco: Ignatius Press, 1996), 21–22.

2. St. Thomas Aquinas, *Summa Theologica,* I–II, 26,4.

3. Pope John Paul II, *Man and Woman He Created Them: A Theology of the Body,* trans. Michael Waldstein (Boston: Pauline Books & Media, 2006), 202–3.

Chapter Two: Four Ears: The Essentials of Communication

1. Address of Pope Francis to Engaged Couples Preparing for Marriage, St. Peter's Square, Friday, 14 February, 2014, www.ccli.org/yls-resources/popefrancis

2. Fr. Erik Pohlmeier, board member and chaplain of the Couple to Couple League, contributed much of the reflection on prayer, including the idea of a daily renewal of vows.

3. National Cursillo Movement, www.ccli.org/yls-resources/cursillo

Chapter Three: Natural Covenant Marriage

1. The idea of sex as a renewal of the marriage covenant appears to have been first developed by John F. Kippley, founder (with his wife, Sheila) of the Couple to Couple League. See John F. Kippley, *Sex and the Marriage Covenant: A Basis for Morality* (Cincinnati, Ohio: The Couple to Couple League, 1991). A revised and expanded version was later published by Ignatius Press. (See resource list.) The biblical basis of covenant, and the idea of marriage as a covenant, is further developed by John S. Grabowski in *Sex and Virtue: An Introduction to Sexual Ethics* (Washington, DC: Catholic University of America Press, 2003).

Chapter Five: Living Together, Banana Milkshakes, and Legal Marriage

1. Shirley S. Wang, "The Tricky Chemistry of Attraction: Taking Birth-Control Pills May Mask the Signals That Draw the Sexes Together, Research Shows," *Wall Street Journal*, updated May 9, 2011, www.ccli.org/yls-resources/shirleywang

2. Karol Wojtyla, *Love and Responsibility*, trans. G. Ignatik (Boston: Pauline Press, 2013).

Chapter Six: "I Do!": Your Journey to the Heart of Marriage

1. "Top 10 Shortest Celebrity Marriages of All Time," Answers.com, www.ccli.org/yls-resources/celebritymarriages

2. With regard to non-sacramental or natural marriage, there are two exceptions to this rule: the Pauline Privilege (sometimes called the Privilege of the Faith) and the Favor or the Faith (sometimes called the Petrine Privilege) The first of these allows under certain circumstances the dissolution of a non-sacramental marriage between two non-Christians, one of whom becomes a Catholic Christian. It is based on the words of St. Paul in 1 Corinthians 7:12–15. The Favor of the Faith is reserved to the Pope, who can grant the dissolution of a valid, non-sacramental marriage if it is deemed appropriate to protect the faith of a Catholic married to an unbaptized person. For more information on the Pauline Privilege, see Code of Canon Law, Canon Law Society of America, Washington, DC, 1999, Can. 1143. For the Petrine Privilege, see the "2001 Instruction from the Congregation for the Doctrine of the Faith: Norms on the Preparation of the Process for the Dissolution of the Marriage Bond in Favour of the Faith," www.ccli.org/yls-resources/canonlaw

3. Again, there are two relatively rare, Bible-based exceptions, the Pauline Privilege and the Favor of the Faith, which allow the dissolution of natural, non-sacramental marriages under certain circumstances. See footnote above.

4. The *Catechism of the Catholic Church*, 1812–1813, says: "The human virtues are rooted in the theological virtues, which adapt man's faculties for participation in the divine nature: for the theological virtues relate directly to God. They dispose Christians to live in a relationship with the Holy Trinity. They have the One and Triune God for their origin, motive, and object.

"The theological virtues are the foundation of Christian moral activity; they animate it and give it its special character. They inform and give life to all the moral virtues. They are infused by God into the souls of the faithful to make them capable of acting as his children and of meriting eternal life. They are the pledge of the presence and action of the Holy Spirit in the faculties of the human being. There are three theological virtues: faith, hope, and charity."

Chapter Seven: The Dance of Courtship

1. Edward Lear, "The Owl and the Pussy-Cat," www.ccli.org/yls-resources/edwardlear

Chapter Eight: Becoming One Flesh: The Twofold Meaning of Sex

1. "The Internet and Pornography," issued by the United States Council of Catholic Bishops, www.ccli.org/yls-resources/usccb And the floodgates have been opened for individuals of all ages: A staggering total of 4.2 million websites contain pornography, with 68 million requests being made daily for pornographic material (see chart on page 18).

2. Steven Swinford, "Most children will be born out of wedlock by 2016," *Telegraph*, July 10, 2013, www.ccli.org/yls-resources/stevenswinford

3. "Divorce . . . permanently weakens the family and the relationship between children and parents. It frequently leads to destructive conflict management methods, diminished social competence and for children, the early loss of virginity, as well as a diminished sense of masculinity or femininity for young adults. It also results in more trouble with dating, more cohabitation, greater likelihood of divorce, higher expectations of divorce later in life, and a decreased desire to have children." Patrick F. Fagan and Aaron Churchill, "The Effects of Divorce on Children," Marri Research, Family Research Council, Washington, DC, January 11, 2012.

4. John F. Kippley, *Sex and the Marriage Covenant: A Basis for Morality* (Cincinnati, Ohio: The Couple to Couple League, 1991), 7.

Chapter Nine: The Seasons of Married Life: Natural Family Planning

1. Encyclical Letter *Humanae Vitae*, www.ccli.org/yls-resources/vatican
   Humanae Vitae: Encyclical Letter of His Holiness Pope Paul VI, a revised, improved translation by Ignatius Press, 2002, www.ccli.org/yls-resources/ignatiuspress

2. See, for example, Robin McKie, "£30bn bill to purify water system after toxic impact of contraceptive pill," *Guardian*, June 2, 2012, www.ccli.org/yls-resources/robinmckie

Chapter Ten: The Sacrament of Marriage and the Life of God

1. The idea for this comparison comes from Fr. Erik Pohlmeier.

2. St. Athanasius, *On the Incarnation*, 54:3, 25:192B; also *Catechism of the Catholic Church*, 460.

Afterword: Live Your Story of Love

1. William Shakespeare, *Romeo and Juliet*, act 2, scene 2, lines 2 and 120.

Supplement: The Rite of Marriage and Readings

1. "Address of Pope Francis to Engaged Couples Preparing for Marriage," St. Peter's Square, Friday, 14 February, 2014, www.ccli.org/yls-resources/popefrancis

Resources

The Couple to Couple League has compiled a list of books, blogs, tools, and online resources, including writings by some of the best and the brightest authors coupled with the wisdom of the Catholic Church. A complete list can be found here: www.ccli.org/yls-resources.

The many insightful resources are systematically grouped into four categories:

- *Love and Marriage*
  (www.ccli.org/yls-resources/loveandmarriage)

- *Sexuality and the Theology of the Body*
  (www.ccli.org/yls-resources/sexuality)

- *Fertility and Natural Family Planning*
  (www.ccli.org/yls-resources/nfp)

- *Prayer, Holy Mass, and Daily Readings*
  (www.ccli.org/yls-resources/prayers)

Acknowledgments

MANY PEOPLE HAVE CONTRIBUTED IN NUMEROUS WAYS to this book, including all of the young couples who have taught my wife and me about the joys and challenges of engagement, while we have taught them about marriage and Natural Family Planning. More than forty people volunteered their time to read the manuscript of this book at various stages and offered their insights and suggestions, including engaged and newly married couples, CCL teaching couples, parish priests, professors of philosophy and theology, and family life directors. Over one hundred people have generously made financial contributions to cover the cost of publication. My heartfelt thanks to you all.

Special thanks are due to Erik Tozzi, Mike Manhart, and the rest of the Couple to Couple League board and staff who guided this project from its inception. Also thanks to Elianne Obadia, The Writer's Midwife, editor par excellence, who demands (sweetly) the best; to Fr. Erik Pohlmeier, who shared so much of his experience and wisdom; to Bob McLoughlin for his tireless work and enthusiasm; to Fr. Joseph Illo for the story of his bicycle ride to sacerdotal destiny; to Sarah Gentner for myriad useful suggestions; to Louis Kolenda for encouragement and advice; to Sr. Marianne Farina and her students at the Dominican School of Philosophy and Theology in Berkeley for their critical comments; to Dr. Herb Hartman for good counsel; to Bill and Nicole Hull for millennial insight; to Fr. Emmanuel Taylor, OP, for support; to

Loretta Rogers for research; to Elissa Rabellino and Jeannie Ewing for proofreading; to Scott Bruno for the interior layout and design, and to Katie and Chris Bystedt for insight and joy.

I am also grateful to Stephen Dudro for his wonderful illustrations, to Maria Marsella for her beautiful cover design, and to Ann Gundlach, Anand Bheemarasetti, and everyone on our production team who took on the responsibilities of project coordination and research. Finally, I want to thank my patient and resourceful wife, Pat, who daily shows me in many ways the beauty of Christian love.

Above all, thanks be to God for helping all of us, who are made in his image, to write our human love stories in the context of his divine and eternal love story.

About the Couple to Couple League

THE COUPLE TO COUPLE LEAGUE (CCL) is an organization dedicated to helping couples build joyful relationships through God's beautiful plan for marriage. CCL teaches a method of birth regulation that is . . .

- **highly effective**

In several independent scientific studies published in major peer-reviewed journals, this method of Natural Family Planning has been rated as being more than 99 percent effective in avoiding conception.

- **completely natural**

CCL recognizes that healthy fertility is a both a gift and a responsibility. Instead of using artificial forms of birth control, which override and repress the way your bodies have been designed to work, you can become joint stewards of your own natural fertility.

- **fully supportive of a deep mutual love and commitment**

Many couples report a surprising flowering of respect and love in their marriage—and couples practicing Natural Family Planning have a drastically lower divorce rate compared with couples using contraception.

The Couple to Couple League can guide you on your journey of discovery. Founded in 1971, CCL is the largest Natural Family Planning provider in the United States and has taught NFP and the beauty of God's plan for marriage to more than four hundred fifty thousand people. A small staff at the headquarters in Cincinnati, Ohio, supports the mission of the league and publishes an award-winning magazine, *Family Foundations*. CCL teaching couples are active in all fifty states and several foreign countries. Classes are available in person and online.

The Couple to Couple League International, Inc.
4290 Delhi Avenue, Cincinnati, OH 45238-5829
www.ccli.org
(513) 471-2000 • (800) 745-8252 • Fax: (513) 557-2449

More from the Couple to Couple League!

NFP Instruction

CCL teaches the Sympto-Thermal Method, a modern, scientific, and highly effective way to postpone or achieve pregnancy. With the guidance of a certified teaching couple, you and your fiancé(é) or spouse will benefit from both their knowledge of the method and experience of using NFP in their own marriage. No matter which form of our class you select, you will receive our first-rate program and ongoing support while learning and beyond.

Live Onsite • Live Online • Self-paced Online
Learn more at ccli.org/learn-nfp-from-ccl/

CyclePro*Go*

CyclePro*Go* is CCL's electronic charting tool and app that interprets charts based on CCL's method rules. Charts and data can be accessed from multiple devices, so husband and wife can both be involved in charting.

CyclePro*Go* allows for recording all fertility symptoms, ovulation test results, fertility monitor readings, weight, notes, and numerous other events, including custom-defined events. You can also share charts with your teacher or friends.

Start your FREE TRIAL by downloading CyclePro*Go* from the app stores.

Family Foundations magazine

CCL's award-winning magazine is unique in highlighting the stories of couples who practice NFP. From the newly married and new-to-NFP, to seasoned veterans who appreciate the impact NFP has had on their marriages, each issue focuses on a theme that touches all NFP couples at one time or another.

Available in digital or print subscriptions.
Visit ccli.org/product-category/magazines/

About the Author

BILL TURRENTINE SERVES AS A DEACON in the Archdiocese of San Francisco. With his wife of thirty-eight years, Patricia, he has helped couples prepare for marriage and has taught Natural Family Planning for over three decades. For four years he was chairman of the board of the Couple to Couple League. While continuing to work at the wine brokerage firm he co-founded, Deacon Bill has been pursuing a second master's degree, this time at the Dominican School of Philosophy and Theology at the Graduate Theological Union in Berkeley. Bill and his wife have been blessed with five sons, three daughters-in-law, and eight of the cutest grandchildren in the world.